The GREATEST
in the WORLD

LEADER

Tony Rossiter

The Greatest
Management
Tips
in the World

952, 308 / 658.002

A 'The Greatest in the World' book

www.thegreatestintheworld.com

Cover images:
© Scott Maxwell; © Dara
both courtesy of www.fotolia.com, © Michael Pearcy

Layout
Shazia Saleemi
www.designspirit.co.uk

Copy editor:
Bronwyn Robertson
www.theartsva.com

Series creator/editor:
Steve Brookes

Published in 2008 by
The Greatest in the World Ltd, PO Box 3182,
Stratford-upon-Avon, Warwickshire CV37 7XW

A CIP catalogue record for this book is available from the British Library
ISBN 978-1-905151-44-8

Printed and bound in Italy by Printer Trento s.r.l.

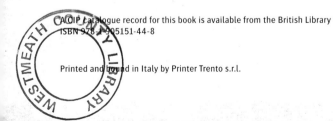

> You can do what I cannot do. I can do what you cannot do. Together we can do great things.

Mother Teresa

Contents

Foreword by Martin Stanley...   7

    Chapter 1   **Managing people**   9

    Chapter 2   **Managing time**   25

    Chapter 3   **Managing presentations**   37

    Chapter 4   **Managing meetings**   53

    Chapter 5   **Managing projects**   69

    Chapter 6   **Managing communication**   83

    Chapter 7   **Managing teams**   99

    Chapter 8   **Managing negotiations**   123

    Chapter 9   **Managing decisions**   135

    Chapter 10   **Managing change**   145

Recommended reading   154

Index   155

The Greatest Tips in the World books & DVDs   158

The author   160

"Never tell people how to do things. Tell them what to do, and they will surprise you with their ingenuity.

General George S. Patton

Foreword by Martin Stanley...

There is no shortage of management books. Look in any bookshop, or go online, and you'll be spoilt for choice. But there are not many books by those who, like Tony Rossiter, have spent their careers at the coalface – not researching or teaching, but dealing with the day-to-day issues and problems faced by any manager.

Drawing on more than 40 years' hands-on experience of management in the UK and overseas, Tony provides tips covering the basic qualities and core competences which any manager, working at any level in any organisation, needs. They are presented clearly and simply, with a light touch, in plain, easy-to-read language.

If you have just moved into your first management job, this book will serve as a concise yet comprehensive primer to keep in your desk drawer and refer to as and when you need it. If you're already an experienced manager, then you will find yourself asking, as you go through the book "when did I last think about this?" And, more importantly, "when did I last put it into practice?" And whether you are experienced or not, you will find it very readable, and to contain much sane, sensible and practical advice.

Martin Stanley

Martin Stanley is Chief Executive of the Competition Commission. He has held senior positions at the Department of Trade and Industry and Cabinet Office, and regularly writes and lectures on management, government and the civil service.

A desk is a dangerous place from which to view the world.

John Le Carré

Managing people
Remember they're all humans

chapter 1
Managing people

What exactly do we mean by management? Different textbooks give different definitions – many are along the lines of "achieving desired goals through planning, organising, directing and controlling." A shorter definition, which I rather like, is "getting results through other people."

An organisation may have an inspiring mission statement, clear goals, a compelling strategy, realistic and challenging work targets, and excellent systems and procedures. But none of these counts for much unless it has enthusiastic, committed people. Handling and motivating people is at the heart of effective management.

For my money people skills are the most important attribute of any manager. Of course, they're not enough on their own. This book covers the core management skills which I believe are needed by anyone operating at any level in any organisation. People skills help you to put them all into practice.

This chapter is about managing people – yourself, your staff, your colleagues, your customers and, last but not least, your boss. Further tips about team-working and managing teams are given in Chapter 7.

Manage by walking about

Management by walking about (MBWA) is one of the best management tools around. If you're closeted in an office, hunched over a desk or have your eyes glued to a computer screen, you won't see half of what's going on.

MBWA is the way to see what's really happening and to find out how people really feel. It also helps your team to see what you're interested in, what your standards are, what you like and what you don't like. You can apply MBWA outside your own team – in other departments and other organisations. Go and see what they are doing! You'll almost certainly learn something.

Network for all you're worth

Do all you can to make contacts and to cultivate informal networks: look beneath the surface and you'll find them everywhere – in your own department, in the rest of the organisation, and in the outside world. The grapevine often tells you more about what is really going on than anyone will dare tell you openly or officially. If you're faced with a particularly difficult problem, the chances are that someone somewhere else will have come up against something similar.

Networking is the way to tap into that kind of informal knowledge and experience. The more networks you are plugged into, the better. Obviously some will be more useful and more reliable than others. Most successful people have an extensive range of personal contacts which they have built up over the years. A good contacts list is worth its weight in gold.

Ask questions – and listen to the answers

Never be afraid to ask questions or to challenge assumptions. The journalist's stock questions are often the best: Why? When? Who? Where? How? What if? Asking the same question of different people is often a good tactic. You can learn a lot from getting different perspectives on the same issue. Once you have asked the question, listen very carefully to the answer. If that sounds obvious, remember that active listening can be hard work, especially if the person answering goes on a bit!

Be old-fashioned

You don't have to know the latest management theories to be an effective manager. Theories and fashions come and go. Most of the important qualities have been around for years and years, and are likely to endure for many more years: things like honesty, integrity, truthfulness, industriousness, reliability, accountability, dedication, loyalty, trustworthiness, determination, resilience and plain common sense.

Enjoy!

Enjoy your work – and help others to enjoy their work. Enthusiasm can be very infectious. Every job ever invented has its lows as well as its highs. There are bound to be some aspects of your work that are less enjoyable than others – and probably some that are no fun at all! But being as enthusiastic and upbeat as you can is a good guiding principle. If you're positive, the chances are that others will follow your example.

Don't say one thing and do another

It's not difficult for a manager to lose the respect of colleagues or staff. All he/she has to do is to tell them one thing, and then to do another. For example, expecting everyone to be in the office by 9 o'clock on the dot, and then rolling up yourself at 10. It's pretty obvious that this won't do much for staff morale, but it's surprising how many senior managers don't make the connection. Remember: deeds speak louder than words.

Don't mislead

Honesty is important. Don't make promises you won't be able to keep. If you have to pass on bad news, don't shirk the responsibility. Choose the right time and the right way to do it. Do it carefully and sensitively. But do it. Occasionally there may be circumstances which prevent you from telling your people as much as you know yourself. If that is the case, just tell them what you can and stop there. They may not like it, but they will like it even less if you mislead them.

And don't double-deal

Don't express one view of an issue to one person and a different view to someone else. That might be expedient in the short term; but in the long term it will do you no good. You'll be regarded as untrustworthy and duplicitous. On the other hand, the way you express your view, and the facts and arguments you use to support it, may well need to vary according to who you are talking to. You'll want to take account of "where they are coming from." In other words, say the same thing to everyone, but say it differently.

"Write and publish what you want, but the only missions, values and ethics that count in your company are those that manifest themselves in the behaviour of all the people, all the time."

Barry Gibbons

Take your job seriously – but not too seriously

You won't be an effective manager if you don't take the job seriously. Meeting your targets, making sure that your team works effectively and efficiently, maintaining high standards, seeking continuous improvement – it's all very important: it's what you're paid for. But it's worth remembering that work is not the be-all and end-all of life. Sometimes the people you're working with will have other things on their mind. Keep a sense of proportion and perspective. Occasionally you'll need to recognise that there are more important things than work.

Have a sense of humour

Management is a serious business, but the most serious subjects on earth sometimes benefit from a little humour. If you doubt that, listen to any House of Commons debate. Having a sense of humour does not mean cracking jokes. And it definitely does not mean laughing at colleagues or making fun of them. Nor does it mean treating serious issues lightly or flippantly. It simply means recognising that you don't need to be deadly serious all the time; taking the opportunity now and again to lighten the mood; and being prepared to see the funny side of things.

Don't be a manager behaving badly

It's easy to be abrupt or offhand or even downright rude towards those around you. Perhaps you're in a bad mood for some reason—it happens to us all—or you've had some bad news, or you've just had one of those days when absolutely everything has gone wrong. Or maybe you're just focussed on the task in hand, striving to meet a tight deadline, and you resent anything and anyone who breaks your concentration. Whatever the reason for your bad behaviour, just stop and think about the effect on other people. If you're having a bad day, don't take it out on those around you.

Be passionate

If you're passionate about your work and really care about what you're doing, some of that passion is bound to rub off on those around you. The chances are that it will help them to believe that what they are doing is worthwhile and can make a real difference to people's lives.

Don't keep your boss in the dark

Don't try to pull the wool over your boss's eyes, or keep him/her in the dark. If there is bad news, be up front about it. If you're not, the chances are that, sooner or later, he/she'll find out about it from someone else anyway. There are few things senior people dislike more than getting a sudden, nasty shock about which they have had no prior warning, even though the unpleasant facts have been known for some time at a lower level in the organisation. Don't keep bad news to yourself.

Your boss's problems are your opportunities

Take time to understand your boss. Get to know what he/she does and why; what pressure he/she is under and where it comes from; what he/she likes and what he/she dislikes; and what he/she finds really annoying! We all have good points and bad points, our strengths and our weaknesses – even the boss.

It's your job to help the boss. If you can make him/her look good, it won't do your relationship any harm. If your own strengths can compensate for some of the boss's weaknesses, that's great: you'll make an excellent team. If your boss has a problem, it's a real opportunity to show how helpful and resourceful you can be. If the boot's on the other foot and you have a problem you need to take to the boss, try not to present it to him/her without suggesting how it can be solved.

If you have a difficult boss, grasp the nettle

No-one is perfect. The chances are you won't like everything your boss does or agree fully with the way he/she operates. Whatever kind of boss you have, you've got to survive and to make the best of it. So you might just have to follow Churchill's advice. KBO – keep buggering on!

If life becomes intolerable and your boss is consistently acting in a way which is unfair or unreasonable, you'll have to do something about it. If you don't and you end up totally stressed out, your health is bound to suffer.

Begin by broaching the matter orally; but before you speak to your boss, make sure you're prepared. Make a note of the points you're going to make and rehearse them – and make sure you're armed with some specific examples. If an oral approach does not work, put your concerns in writing and consider copying your note to your boss's boss: if whatever you are complaining about is happening consistently, he/she may already have heard about it. Your complaint might confirm existing suspicions and convince him/her of the need to take action. Stranger things have happened.

Learn how to influence and persuade

Whether you're dealing with your staff, colleagues, customers or your boss, influencing and persuading is an important management skill. There are usually four key stages:

- Make sure you thoroughly understand the case you're making: be clear in your own mind about the facts and the arguments.

- Check that your facts are 100% accurate and make sure that your arguments really stand up.

- Put yourself in the shoes of the person(s) you're seeking to influence or persuade. That will help you to decide what approach to take and which facts and arguments to use.

- Put your points across (whether orally or in writing) as clearly and concisely as you can.

Get yourself a mentor

A mentor is usually a senior colleague, whom you trust and whose advice you respect, who agrees to act as an informal adviser and counsellor. Few people can resist responding when their views are sought, and senior managers often find it rewarding to help younger talent. A good mentor should be able to help with almost anything, from the detailed and trivial to the strategic. The mentor's role is private and confidential.

Have a personal plan

Instead of making a New Year's resolution, make a career-related resolution. One well known politician is said to have sketched out his life plan on the back of a cigarette packet while at university. He set out his goals, the last of which saw him arriving as Prime Minister at 10, Downing Street. He didn't quite make it, but perhaps it was not such a bad idea. Your goals will probably be rather different, but you can apply the same principle: set your sights high and have a clear objective.

It's easy to live only in the here and now. A personal plan, perhaps setting out where you aim to be in five or ten years' time, can help to keep your managerial career on track. Keep it to yourself, in case it does not fit with how others see your future. 952, 308 | 658·002

Get to know them

The better you know someone, the easier it is to get on with them (OK, there might be the odd exception!). Make a real effort to get to know the people you work with. Take an interest in their families and their lives outside the office. Who knows, you might discover a mutual passion for renaissance art – or the Bactrian camels of Mongolia! An occasional get-together after work, with an opportunity to talk to people in a less stuffy, more relaxed environment, can be good for building personal relationships – and even for getting to grips with some work-related problem that is too sensitive to discuss in the office.

Be yourself

Don't pretend to be someone you're not. Trying to change your personality to suit what you think the organisation wants is almost certainly doomed to failure. The best approach is to understand yourself and your preferred working style(s) as clearly as you can, perhaps using one of the personality profiling models mentioned in Chapter 7. If you really know yourself (how you relate to others, how you deal with information, how you tackle problems) you should be able to adapt your approach to accommodate the needs of those you're working with.

Say what you think

There may still be a few top managers around who like their subordinates to carry out their wishes without question. But most organisations today value managers who think for themselves. Don't be afraid to say what you think – provided, of course, that you have the facts and the arguments to back up your opinion. Once your views have been heard and a decision has been taken, it's your job as a manager to implement that decision, even if you don't like it.

Don't micro-manage

The more you can let people manage both themselves and their own work, the better. Don't be afraid to let go. You need to keep an eye on things, of course; to make sure that things are running smoothly and that people are on course to meet their targets. But if you can't see the wood for the trees, you're never going to be an effective manager.

Don't lose your temper

Of course, you're allowed to be angry. If someone makes a bad mistake, or fails to carry out an important task, you're going to be very annoyed. That's human nature: it's what you'd expect of any manager who cares about the reputation of his/her unit and its ability to deliver the goods. If something has gone wrong, you need to find out exactly what happened and why – and to do your damnedest to make sure it does not happen again. But all this is best done when you are in a calm, cool frame of mind and you can address the issues clearly and objectively. Losing your temper will not help.

Be fair-minded and even-handed

We're all human, and we all like some people more than others. But a manager won't be fully effective if he/she is seen to treat some people better than others. Put personal preferences and prejudices aside and deal with your colleagues and staff fairly and even-handedly. If you treat people unfairly you won't get the best out of them.

Avoid a blame culture

Don't blame people – especially not in public. It's never, ever a good idea to humiliate someone or undermine their self-respect. It's always better to build people up rather than knock them down. A blame culture is unhealthy – and it won't help you to achieve results.

Don't be afraid of the top team

However senior your colleagues are, remember that they are just fallible human beings like the rest of us. Just like you, they have to get out of bed in the morning, wash, dress, eat, drink, urinate and do everything else human beings do. If you're meeting the CEO or MD for the first time, try not to be overawed. He/she won't eat you alive.

Listen to your customers

Remember that your customers are people too. In dealing with them, use the same people skills you use when dealing with your colleagues and your staff. Pay attention to what they tell you. Feedback from those who use what you produce—whether that's a computer programme, an investment portfolio or an internal report—is the best way of making sure you are providing what the customer wants. If you always put the customer first, your management decisions are unlikely to go far wrong.

Customers are not all the same

Different customers have different needs. What satisfies one may not satisfy another. Remember that your customers are individuals, with individual likes and dislikes. That may mean adapting the way you and your team work. Remember that the customer's needs are more important than your own convenience.

Chapter summary

- Any manager operating at any level in any organisation needs the core skills and competences described in this book.

- Handling and motivating people is at the heart of effective management.

- People skills enable you to put into practice all the other competences which every manager needs.

- Network to build up an extensive range of personal contacts.

- Don't be afraid to ask questions and challenge assumptions.

- Pay attention to old-fashioned virtues such as honesty, integrity and accountability.

- Don't say one thing and do another.

- Remember that your boss's problems are your opportunities.

- Map out a personal career plan with a clear objective.

- Make a real effort to get to know the people you work with.

> **As I grow older I pay less attention to what men say. I just watch what they do.**

Andrew Carnegie

Managing time
There's never enough

chapter 2
Managing time

Time is limited: it doesn't last for ever. We need to make the best use of it we can – whether we're thinking about the amount of time we have left on earth, how we're going to spend the weekend, or how we use our time at work.

The need to control or reduce costs is a fact of corporate life, and staff salaries are often the biggest single cost. Cost-cutting, perhaps involving an increased use of technology and a flatter management structure, can mean fewer people doing more work. Salary costs have to be balanced against each person's contribution to the organisation. A manager's time is too expensive to waste.

Time management is one of the most important of all management skills. It involves planning and prioritising, knowing how and when (and when not) to delegate, and avoiding procrastination. It means being in control – being more proactive and less reactive.

Effective time management requires a clear focus on the results you're seeking to achieve; resistance to distractions and irrelevancies which get in the way and don't help you to achieve your objectives; and controlling each day's agenda so that you make the best possible use of the time available.

It's easy to waste time – don't do it!

It's so easy: there are so many ways of wasting time. Reading stuff we don't need to read. Constantly checking our email inbox. Surfing the net to check the football results or the winning lottery numbers. Going to meetings we don't need to go to. Phoning or texting our friends. Chatting to colleagues about things we don't really need to discuss. Spending time on inconsequential stuff because it's so much easier than tackling the difficult task we should really be getting to grips with. I could go on...

Remember the 80:20 rule

Have you heard of the Pareto principle? Pareto was an Italian economist who lived in the early 1900s. He observed that about 20% of the people controlled or owned 80% of the country's wealth. In the 1940s a quality management pioneer working in the United States, Dr Joseph Juran, realised that the same principle was applicable to almost any aspect of management.

Let me explain this with a couple of examples. On a production line, 20% of product defects typically cause 80% of the problems; and 80% of a company's revenue typically comes from sales made by 20% of the sales force.

Importantly for any manager, focussing on just 20% of the work is likely to produce 80% of the results. The trick, therefore, is to identify and spend most of your effort on that critical 20%. If you're able to do that, the chances are you'll see a big improvement in your effectiveness.

Concentrate on the vital 20%

So spend most of your time, your energy and your creative thinking dealing with that vital 20% of your work that will probably account for 80% of your outcomes. This should mean focussing on those work objectives and targets that are most important to your organisation, to your boss and (last but not least) to your own career prospects. It means doing the big things well.

Ask yourself: is it urgent or important?

If you're faced with a new task, ask yourself two simple questions. Firstly, is it urgent? Secondly, is it important? If it's both urgent and important, do it as soon as you can. If it's urgent but not important, get one of your team to do it. If it's important but not urgent, you can do it later. If it's neither urgent nor important, don't do it!

Be clear about your priorities

If you have several tasks that are both urgent and important, you need to prioritise your priorities, and that may not be easy.

During recent management training seminars in Moldova and in Kosovo, officials in both countries told me that it was impossible to rank their priorities. "Everything is a priority" they said, quite sincerely. "But if everything is a priority" I pointed out "what that means in practice is that nothing is a priority."

If you have lots of important tasks on your plate, prioritising these can be painful. Think carefully about the criteria you use.

Set yourself deadlines

I'm a great believer in setting deadlines – both for others and for myself. If you have several tasks to do, write down the date by which you'll aim to complete each one. The date needs to be realistic but reasonably challenging. If it's too generous you may find yourself falling prey to Parkinson's Law: "Work expands so as to fill the time available for its completion." A deadline concentrates the mind. Without a copy deadline *The Greatest Management Tips in the World* would not have been written.

Write a "to do" list

Begin each day by jotting down a list of things you aim to get through. For some, you might want to write down not just the task (e.g. chair staff meeting) but also the outcome you hope to achieve (e.g. persuade them that the CEO is not such a bad guy). Inevitably, your plan will sometimes be thrown out of kilter by an unforeseen crisis or by a boss who believes that his/her deadlines are more important than yours; but that's life.

Keep you priorities under review

It's important to review your priorities regularly. The world does not stand still. Remember that you're operating in a constantly changing environment. What was a top priority at the beginning of the year may become less important a few months—or even a few days—later, for all kinds of reasons. There might be changes in the political or economic environment or in your organisation's policies or personnel. There may be new developments or an unforeseen crisis which has to be dealt with. Make sure that your priorities reflect the current reality.

The first percept
was never to accept a
thing as true until I
knew it was without
a single doubt.

René Descartes

Don't be too reactive

Don't be too reactive to the demands of others. You yourself must decide how you spend your time. Be clear about what it is you have to do, and make sure you're in the driving seat. Remember that your boss will judge you on the work you produce and the results you achieve. So concentrate, first and foremost, on meeting your own objectives and targets.

If you're the kind of person who likes to be helpful to colleagues (and most of us are), discipline yourself to put your own interests first. By all means be helpful to others, but resist any requests that get in the way of your own priorities.

It's important to be in control of your own work. Be single-minded: be clear about your priorities, and make sure that you devote most of your time and energy to those tasks which are most important to you.

Handle each piece of paper only once: be DAFT

It's easy to waste time by having to reread a paper you read a few days ago without deciding what to do with it. Try to handle each piece of paper only once. There are really only four ways of dealing with it:

- **D**elegate it
- **A**ct on it yourself
- **F**ile it away for future reference
- **T**hrow it away

Take action

If you need to take action on it yourself, try to do it straight away. Occasionally you may get an important paper which you do really need to look at carefully, but cannot deal with immediately. You might be doing something that's even more urgent and important. In that case, it's sensible to put it aside until you have the time to look at it properly. But if you do that, make sure you read it and deal with it as soon as you possibly can.

The next time a paper lands on your desk, don't just read it and put it aside. Decide what to do with it. Remember DAFT.

Don't go to every meeting

For some managers, meetings are a way of life. They may even enjoy them, perhaps seeing them as a far pleasanter way of spending time than getting to grips with the pile of difficult stuff they should really be tackling. Even the most conscientious manager may welcome the excuse to have a break away from the desk.

Remember that you don't need to go to every meeting to which you are invited. Attending meetings can become a (bad) habit and take up an enormous chunk of your time. If you're asked to go to a meeting, ask yourself whether or not it will help you to achieve your own work objectives. If it won't —and unless there is some other objective reason which justifies your attendance— don't go!

Hide yourself away

If you're faced with a particularly tricky task, mark off a time-slot in your diary when you won't be available to others. Find somewhere quiet away from colleagues where you won't be disturbed, such as a meeting room that's not being used. Or you may be able to work at home, or in a quiet corner of your favourite pub or café. And give yourself an incentive. Resolve that you won't leave (or have lunch or go to bed) until you have completed the task.

Don't read everything

Despite IT and wishful thinking about the paperless office, most organisations produce lots of paper. Don't read everything that lands on your desk. The heading will often be enough to tell you that it can go straight into the waste paper basket. If you do need to look at it, you can probably skim through. Look out for key headings: summary, conclusions, recommendations, action points. You're probably quite discriminating when it comes to leisure reading. Apply the same self-discipline at work. Only read what will help you to do your job or develop your career.

Take a break!

However busy you are, it's not a good idea to slog away at your desk for hour after hour without a break. If you do that, the quality of your work is bound to suffer. If you have to grab a sandwich at your desk for lunch, at least get out of the office for half an hour to stretch your legs and get some fresh air.

Be punctual

It doesn't matter whether you're meeting a VIP or having a routine meeting with your team. Make a habit of being on time. If you're late, you're implicitly telling people that your own time and convenience are more important than theirs.

If you're chairing a meeting, begin on time and don't wait for anyone who is late. If you do, you'll be wasting not only your own time, but that of everyone who has made the effort to be punctual.

Senior people who habitually keep others waiting may believe that this enhances their own importance. All it does is show a lack of consideration for others. Of course, an unforeseen crisis can prevent anyone from being on time, but that should be the exception.

Energy can get you to the top

There is no substitute for energy and hard work. That's how you can make the best possible use of your time. Those who make it to the top of any organisation are usually intelligent individuals with good communication skills and a clear focus on results. But there is something else that is at least as important – sheer energy. Look at any sphere of activity—sport, politics, the arts, the media, business—and you'll see that those who reach the very top often have no more talent or intelligence than their peers. What sets them apart, more often than not, is sheer energy and drive. Energy can take you a long way.

Chapter summary

- Focus on the vital 20% of your work that will probably account for 80% of your outcomes.

- Do the big things well.

- Faced with a new task, ask yourself:
  Is it urgent? Is it important?

- Set deadlines, for yourself and for others, which are challenging but realistic.

- Write a daily "to do" list.

- Prioritise your priorities.

- Handle each piece of paper only once.

- Faced with a tricky task, find a quiet place and a time when you won't be available to others.

- Be punctual.

- Energy and drive can get you to the top.

Good management is the art of making problems so interesting and their solutions so constructive that everyone wants to get to work and deal with them.

Paul Hawken

Managing presentations

How to make an impact
(and keep the audience awake)

chapter 3
Managing presentations

If you're not used to it, it can be a nerve-racking experience: having to stand up in front of a group of people and make a presentation. It's natural to have a few butterflies — especially if you have just moved into a new job or you are faced with a large or an unfamiliar audience.

It's important to do your homework: the better prepared you are, the more confident you'll feel. Make sure you're clear about the purpose of the presentation and the expectations of the audience. Get to grips thoroughly with the subject-matter, and give careful thought both to the content and to the structure of what you're going to say.

Preparation is the key: if you're well prepared, you'll find it easier to relax and to be yourself. Try to approach the task in a positive frame of mind. The truth is that the audience will want you to do well. You have something useful to say and they want to hear it. They haven't come along to catch you out! Don't think defensively or imagine that you need to have every conceivable fact and figure at your fingertips. Just focus on the essentials and on putting those across as clearly as you can.

Making a presentation can be a great opportunity to get known and to make an impact on people. Make the most of it. Believe it or not, if you have prepared thoroughly and you know exactly why you're making the presentation and what you want to achieve, you may find yourself looking forward to it.

Focus on the audience

Before you begin preparing your presentation, take time to think about the audience. If you don't already know them, you'll need to do some research. Who are they? Where are they from? How many of them are there? Why are they attending? How much experience do they have? What is their interest likely to be? How much do they already know about the subject? What will they want to know? What are their expectations? What do they want to get out of it? You need to answer all these questions before you begin to think about the content of your presentation.

Talk to them beforehand

Most people feel more relaxed when they are talking to people they know. So a presentation to a small group of colleagues you work closely with and know quite well is likely to be less stressful than a presentation to a large room full of strangers. I always find that it helps if there are at least a few familiar faces in the audience. And if there is an opportunity to chat to a few people beforehand, that's an added bonus. Sometimes it can give you a last-minute clue about what the audience is hoping to get out of the presentation. More importantly, exchanging an informal word or two with a few people before you begin can transform an impersonal mass of humanity into real human beings with individual feelings and foibles. You'll probably find that they are easier to talk to, and more receptive to hearing what you're going to say, than you had imagined.

Make sure you know why you're making the presentation

It may sound obvious, but it's important to be crystal clear about the purpose of your presentation. Are you simply conveying information? Or reporting on something that's happened? Or explaining a new initiative or a new policy? Or seeking to persuade your audience to a particular point of view? Or urging them to take action of some kind? There are many possible reasons for making a presentation. Whatever it is, the important thing is to be clear about it.

Get your aims and objectives down on paper

Write yourself a one-sentence explanation of why you're making the presentation and what you're seeking to achieve. Make sure that your aims and objectives are clear and specific. Put yourself in the shoes of the audience, and frame your objectives from the audience's perspective. For example, a presentation about a new staff assessment system might have the following audience-based aims:

1. to have a clear understanding of the rationale for the new system;

2. to be able to explain to staff the key principles and the main stages in the annual assessment process; and

3. to be able to apply the new system with effect from (say) 1 January.

Think about the setting

Next, think about the setting for your presentation. Will you be addressing half a dozen colleagues in your office? Or two hundred people in a conference room? Or something in between? In planning your presentation you'll need to take account of the environment in which you'll be working.

If you're not already familiar with the room, it's worthwhile checking it out in advance if you possibly can (especially if it's a big occasion). Look at the seating arrangements and try out the sightlines. If you're going to be using visual aids, check what equipment is available and make sure you know how to operate it. Fumbling around in front of your audience searching for the right control switch is unprofessional, wastes time and damages your credibility.

Think about the method

Consider how you can get your message across most effectively. At one extreme, you may decide to speak informally, perhaps eschewing all technical aids and simply using a few notes (or even just key words) to remind yourself of the ground you need to cover. At the other end of the spectrum, you might have to make a formal speech to a large audience – in which case you'll probably need to write it all out in full, and to read it out, either from a copy on the lectern in front of you or from an autocue. Most presentations fall somewhere between these two extremes.

Don't read it out

With the sole exception of a formal speech to a large audience, it's never a good idea to read a presentation. If you are constantly looking down at your script, it's very difficult to maintain eye contact with the audience. Moreover, reading out a prepared text word for word can give the impression (albeit unfairly) that you lack confidence or don't know the subject as well as you should. And, since we don't speak in the same way as we write, it can also make the speaker seem stilted and insincere. It's very much better to prepare speaking notes and to use those to remind yourself of the points you're going to make.

Use what works best for you

There are three main ways of preparing speaking notes:

- Write headlines or key points on a sheet of paper.
- Use cue cards, again with headlines or key points.
- Write structured notes: these can include not only headlines or key points, but also essential facts and figures, arguments, examples and anecdotes.

Each method has its pros and cons. Writing just headlines or key points allows for natural delivery, flexibility and interaction with the audience. If you use this method you'll need to be very familiar with the subject-matter. This applies also to cue cards, which can be held easily in the hands and are therefore useful if you're going to be standing or moving around. The main disadvantage of both these methods is the risk that you won't have all the details you need.

Structured notes enable you to have more information to hand. One refinement of this method is to use a highlighter pen to differentiate the material that's essential from that which is merely desirable. Then, if you are running short of time, it will be easy for you to skip all the non-essential stuff.

I personally like to use cue cards, but I usually expand these to include not just key points but also a few memory joggers – often to remind me of specific examples or anecdotes I'm going to use.

With trial and error you'll discover which method works best for you.

Maintain eye contact

Eye contact is important. A presentation is a form of communication, and communication is a two-way process. Eye contact enables you to check that the information you are giving is being received. If people are yawning or staring at the ceiling, it's a fair bet that you are not exactly grabbing their attention.

Don't just concentrate on one person or on one part of the audience. Look around, towards the back of the room and in the middle as well as at the front row. Try to spend a few seconds looking at different people in different parts of the room. This helps to draw people in and shows that you are speaking to the whole audience.

Consider visual aids

People take in information much more readily through their eyes than through their ears. If you listen to a lecture, the chances are that you'll remember one or two bits of what you're told, but you'll forget a great deal of it. However, if you see a visual image—whether it's an object, a drawing, a photograph, a video clip or a PowerPoint presentation—you're more likely to remember it. One picture can be worth a thousand words, and visuals aids can help to arouse and maintain interest. They won't always be useful or appropriate, but they can often help to get the message across.

A flip chart can be ideal

If your presentation is short, informal, addressed to just a few people, and deals with a subject that is pretty straightforward, a PowerPoint presentation probably won't be appropriate. You might nevertheless want to reinforce or illustrate one or two key points, and in these circumstances a flip chart or a whiteboard can be very useful. If you prepare it beforehand you won't have to waste time or to turn your back on the audience, during the presentation itself. Make sure that your handwriting is legible, and that it can be read by those at the back of the room. A flipchart is ideal for small groups – and, of course, it's particularly useful for capturing ideas and suggestions from the audience and for brainstorming sessions.

PowerPoint can be effective, but use it carefully

PowerPoint can be a very effective and powerful tool, but it needs to be used carefully and correctly. Two key points to remember:

- limit the number of slides;
- limit the number of words on each slide.

As a very rough guide, allow two or three minutes per slide. So if you're making a 20-minute presentation, you probably won't need more than about eight slides. And don't put too much information on each slide: a heading and five spaced-out bullet points, each with no more than six words of text, is ideal. Don't be tempted to read from the screen, and remember to switch the machine off when it's not being used: a glaring white light distracts the audience.

Don't fall for the tyranny of PowerPoint

Don't think of PowerPoint as the automatic choice for any presentation. It is often over-used. If your presentation includes charts, maps, images or other graphical material, PowerPoint will probably be appropriate. If, however, you are speaking to a small audience and your material consists mainly of words, a talk book may be more effective. You can give each person a copy of the book and simply talk them through the key points.

Be cautious about using video

A short video extract can sometimes be useful, for example to add emotional impact to a message or to illustrate a complex process; but if you're not careful it can become a barrier between the speaker and the audience. Use sparingly – only in short sequences and only to explain or illustrate specific points.

Have a plan B

Whatever method of presentation you choose, it's always sensible to have an alternative up your sleeve – just in case, for example, the PowerPoint equipment does not work or the promised flip-chart fails to materialise. Don't risk getting caught out by hiccups of this kind – it's embarrassing and unprofessional. The simplest plan B is often to come along armed with prepared notes which will enable you to stand up on your hind legs and talk to the audience.

Twenty minutes is plenty

Twenty minutes should be long enough for any presentation. That's about as much as most audiences can take. The attention span of most people is surprisingly short. On average it tails off after about eight minutes. After that, they begin to lose interest or switch off entirely. Introducing variety—a visual aid, an anecdote, or a question to the audience—can help to maintain interest. But if you see closed eye-lids or just bored, vacant expressions, you'll know that it's time to sit down.

Take care how you begin and end

For any presentation, the audience's attention is at a peak at the beginning, when they're imagining (perhaps optimistically!) that they're about to hear a brilliant speaker giving a stimulating talk on a riveting subject. After the first minute or two, interest will begin to flag. People will perk up again at the end, when you've signalled that you're about to finish and they're looking forward to the coffee break or the lunch. So take particular care about how you begin and how you end your presentation.

Begin with a remark that draws the audience in and makes it easy for them to relate to you and to what you're about to say. Don't try to be Lenny Henry. Humour is a funny (peculiar), quite personal thing. Something that strikes you as hilarious might fall as flat as a pancake. Just explain, in no more than a couple of sentences, what you're going to be talking about and how it relates to their particular needs. And then make your key points: no more than three or four – that's as many as most people will remember. If you can do all that within the first five minutes, there's a good chance that you'll have grabbed their attention.

When you're near the end, say something to make it clear that you're about to finish (e.g. "before we adjourn for coffee...", "in conclusion...", "before I sit down, let me just..."). With any luck, that signal will make people sit up and take notice of your concluding remarks. Try to end on a strong, positive note.

Remember the rule of three

It sounds corny, but it's nevertheless pretty good advice: tell them what you're going to tell them; then tell them; then tell them what you've told them. As every politician knows, repetition is a good way of ramming home any message. Of course, if you're saying essentially the same thing three times over, it's best to do it in slightly different ways and to use different words.

If you've got three key points to get across, mention them briefly in your introduction, explain and elaborate on them in the main part of your presentation and, finally, reiterate them in your conclusion.

Use specific examples and anecdotes

In the main part of your presentation you'll need to explain and elaborate on your key points. You'll need to give facts and figures, but it's very important to reinforce and illustrate these with specific examples or anecdotes. These add human interest and bring any presentation to life. And they are much more likely to be remembered than dry statistics.

Make good use of questions

Many speakers are at their best when answering questions — they come across more naturally and convincingly. So don't be afraid to invite questions. Make it clear at the outset whether you're prepared to take them during the presentation or only at the end. Then deal with them honestly and thoughtfully. Be brief and to the point. If you don't know the answer, say so: don't waffle or guess.

If the question is unclear, make sure that you and the rest of the audience understand it. This can often be done by paraphrasing it back to the speaker. If you're unlucky enough to be faced with someone who is difficult or obstreperous, just be firm and polite.

Have a rehearsal

There are three ways to rehearse a presentation:

- into a dictating machine;
- in front of a mirror;
- in front of a colleague or friend or partner who is prepared to give constructive feedback.

A rehearsal is the only way to time a presentation accurately, and it is usually time well spent. Don't imagine that a short presentation does not need rehearsing: this can be harder to give, and can require more careful preparation, than a long talk.

Don't speak too quickly

If you're slightly nervous, or if you feel you have a lot of ground to cover and not much time in which to cover it, you might find yourself speaking rather quickly. Almost certainly, this will make it difficult for the audience to follow and take in what you are saying. So make a conscious effort to slow down. Project your voice, vary the tone, emphasise key words and phrases, and speak a little more slowly than normal. If you can do that, your words will gain added weight and authority.

Features of bad presentaion

- Speaker goes on too long.
- Poor delivery (e.g. reads it out, no eye contact, monotone).
- No real grasp of subject-matter.
- Content is not related to the audience's specific needs.
- Packs in too much information.
- Confused or illogical structure.
- Too much or too little detail.
- No opportunity to comment or ask questions.
- Bad use of visual aids (e.g. slides with too much text).
- Equipment problems.
- Unconvincing body language.
- Inappropriate dress.
- Inappropriate jokes or humour.
- Lacking energy and conviction.
- Responds to questions by waffling.
- Makes questioner look foolish.
- Loses thread of argument.
- Overweening or arrogant attitude.
- Superficial treatment of issues.
- Tells audience only what they already know.

Don't put on an act

Don't try to take on an alien persona for the benefit of your audience. You're not an actor. Pretending to be someone you're not just does not work. Be as natural as you can and let your own personality come through. Whatever that is, it's sure to go down much better with the audience than any attempt to be someone else.

Chapter summary

- Prepare thoroughly for the presentation.
- Take time to focus on the audience.
- Be clear about the purpose of the presentation.
- Frame yourself some audience-based objectives.
- Don't read the presentation – use speaking notes.
- Consider visual aids.
- Twenty minutes is long enough for any presentation.
- Take especial care over the beginning and the ending.
- Use specific examples and anecdotes.
- Take questions – and deal with them honestly.

Management is efficiency in climbing the ladder of success; leadership determines whether the ladder is leaning against the right wall.

Stephen R. Covey

Managing meetings

They don't have to be long and boring

chapter 4
Managing meetings

If you work an 8-hour day and you have 2 hour-long meetings every day, that's a quarter of your working life spent in meetings. Over a 40-year career that adds up to more than 20,000 hours of meetings. That's more than two years of your life! OK, I'm exaggerating a little: you'll probably get a few meeting-free weeks. It's still a hell of a lot.

Meetings can be useful for doing all kinds of things; they can also be a complete waste of time. Quite often there are more effective and more efficient ways of dealing with things.

It's very easy to have a bad meeting – one that leaves the participants feeling frustrated, resentful of the time they have wasted, and unclear about the outcome. We have all attended meetings like that. If you want to have a good meeting, there are three simple rules:

- Make sure that you really do need to have the meeting – that it's the best way of dealing with the matter.
- Be clear about the purpose – what you're seeking to achieve.
- Prepare thoroughly.

Understand why you're having the meeting

The first essential of any meeting is to be clear—and to make sure that others are clear—about the purpose. Why are you having a meeting? There are many possible reasons. To pass on or obtain information. To seek views. To identify possible ways of dealing with a problem. To take a decision. To get people to take action. To persuade people to support a particular point of view. To resolve differences of opinion. To review progress or plan future work. Whatever it is, the first imperative is to be clear about why you're having the meeting.

Make sure you need a meeting

OK, you're clear about the purpose of the meeting. Before you push ahead with the arrangements, just spare a moment or two to double-check that a meeting really is the best way of dealing with the matter. Could it be dealt with more effectively and more efficiently by some other means? Perhaps by sending out an email? Or making a few phone calls? Or even popping round to have a chat, face to face, with the key people involved? Make sure you really do need a meeting.

Prepare thoroughly

Once you're quite sure that you need to have a meeting and you're crystal clear about the purpose, you can begin your preparation. First, identify the key people – those whose presence is essential. Then think about others with an interest who ought to be invited. Fix the date, time and venue. Consider what background papers or other information the participants will need to have in advance of the meeting.

Most importantly, consider what outcome you hope to achieve. If the purpose is to take a decision or to seek support for a particular course of action, you may well need to prepare the ground beforehand, perhaps by speaking to the key people.

Get the papers out in good time

It's important that those who're attending the meeting receive the agenda and any reports or other papers they need in plenty of time. Above all, avoid giving participants the papers only when they arrive at the meeting – it wastes time and reduces your chances of having an effective meeting. The participants will spend all their time reading the papers instead of listening and contributing to the discussion. And if the papers contain a lot of new information on which you're seeking comments, people may decline to express a view until they have had an opportunity to study the detail. You can hardly blame them.

Don't forget the boring logistics

Participants can easily get hacked off if the organisation goes awry. Little hiccups can have a disproportionate effect on the mood of any meeting. If people are irritated they are less likely to make a constructive contribution. So make sure that everything runs like clockwork.

Check out the room and the seating arrangements. Make sure that any technical equipment is in place and is working properly. Make sure everyone knows when and where the meeting is being held and how to get there. If people are coming from outside the building, make sure the reception and security people know who to expect, and that any necessary passes have been organised. Lay on tea and coffee (or at least water) and notepaper. It's all very basic stuff, but if any one of these little things is overlooked, it can jeopardise the entire meeting. I've seen it happen!

Discourage distractions

Don't let people use mobile phones during the meeting: it's impolite and unprofessional, and will irritate other participants. Use of laptops, Blackberrys and PDAs (personal data assistants) is becoming increasingly common. Encourage anyone who uses these during the meeting to do so with consideration for other participants.

If an exceptionally long meeting is unavoidable, make sure there are periodic comfort or coffee breaks. These will allow people to check messages or make a quick phone call.

Take care how you open the meeting

It's vital to get the meeting off to a good start. The opening comments from the chair are critically important.
He/she needs to:

- welcome participants and make them feel comfortable;

- set the tone – show that the meeting will be conducted in a businesslike manner;

- demonstrate that he/she has a grasp of the subject matter;

- explain the purpose of the meeting and make sure that everyone understands what he/she is expected to contribute;

- explain the ground rules – the timeframe, handling of the agenda, how questions will be dealt with, and so on.

"
When people talk,
  listen completely.
Most people
    never listen.
"

Ernest Hemingway

Help people to feel comfortable

People are more likely to make a constructive contribution if they feel at ease. So it's worth taking the trouble not only to introduce yourself to any participants you don't know, but also to make everyone feel welcome and, in particular, to introduce any newcomer(s). It's always a good idea for the person in the chair to arrive a few minutes early so that he/she can exchange an informal word or two with people before the meeting begins. Even if these exchanges are just about the weather or England's latest football/rugby/cricket fiasco, they can help to break the ice and set the scene for a friendly, constructive discussion.

Don't bully people to accept your own point of view

Sometimes you will have formed your own view, beforehand, of the conclusion you want the meeting to come to or the decision you want it to take. Take care not to alienate participants by pushing your own view too strongly. It's often good tactics to save your own comments until others have had an opportunity to speak. And getting someone else (either a member of your own team or another participant) to articulate a strongly held view of your own can be an effective way of getting your point across without making people feel that you are taking unfair advantage of your role in the chair.

If you want to make sure that your own view prevails without antagonising participants, bend over backwards to ensure that those with opposing views are given the opportunity to make their case. Use facts and arguments to win them over.

Be polite and courteous – and don't put people on the spot

Chairing a meeting is an excellent opportunity to demonstrate your interpersonal skills. You need to treat participants with courtesy and consideration. But you also need to be firm and businesslike. You may need to shut some people up, and to encourage others to open their mouths! It's important to make sure that the meeting is not dominated by one or two opinionated characters who like the sound of their own voices. Sometimes the quietest people have the best ideas. You need to keep the meeting on track, and to discourage over-long or irrelevant interventions. You need to make sure that everyone has an opportunity to express their views, but don't embarrass people or put them on the spot.

Summarise, clarify, question

One of the most important chairing skills is the ability to make sense of incomprehensible contributions! Summarising a long and boring intervention in two or three crisp sentences helps everyone to follow the discussion – and to stay awake.

To summarise what someone has said you need to make a brief note of the key points, and then to regurgitate these using clear, simple language. If someone uses jargon or technical terms that won't be understood by others, ask them to spell it out in everyday language. If something is said that is not clear, it's the chair's job to clarify it. This can often be done by asking the speaker to repeat what has been said, or by rehearsing it back using simpler language ("If I understand you correctly, what you're saying is...").

And if someone makes a dubious statement or assertion, don't hesitate to interrupt and ask for some supporting evidence. Summarise, clarify and question: if you're in the chair, that's your job.

Take care over how you bring the meeting to an end

The chair's concluding remarks are what people will be left with, and it's vital to get them right. The precise content obviously depends on the type of meeting, on how successful it has been, and on the outcome. But at virtually any meeting the person in the chair should:

- summarise the main points of the discussion;
- take especial care to identify any conclusions reached, recommendations agreed or decisions taken;
- go over any agreed action points, making clear exactly what action has to be taken, by whom, and by when;
- set out any next steps (such as another meeting!);
- thank participants for their attendance and end on an upbeat, positive note.

Don't forget to record it

If you don't record what has been agreed and who is to take what follow-up action, it will be difficult to chase up people if they do not do what has been agreed. You need some kind of written record, but the style depends very much on the type of meeting.

There are three main options:

- Action points only: for an informal meeting with your own team (perhaps to discuss an ongoing project or a forthcoming event) a simple list of action points may well be sufficient. List each action point, if necessary adding a sentence to describe exactly what will be done, and against it put the name of the person responsible and the deadline. Simple.

- Detailed record: at the other end of the spectrum, for a major conference you may well need a detailed record, attributing comments to individual speakers.

- Summary record: many meetings fall somewhere between these two extremes, and for these a summary record is often the best option. This summarises the main points made during the discussion (usually without attributing these to individuals) and sets out, as appropriate, the conclusion(s) reached, recommendations made, decisions taken, and action points agreed.

Remember the housekeeping points

The record you decide upon should include details of when and where the meeting was held, who chaired it, who attended and which organisations or departments they represented. It's important to record the names and contact details (telephone numbers and email addresses) of all participants (one way of collating these is on a piece of paper circulated during the meeting). This will make it easy if, after the meeting, the note-taker needs to clarify something that was said, seek additional information, or chase up action points.

Get someone to take a note of the meeting

Nominate someone to take a note of the meeting. The more familiar he/she is with the subject matter, the easier he/she will find it to follow and make sense of the discussion. So if it's a subject new to the note-taker, he/she should be encouraged to prepare by reading the relevant papers. The note-taker needs to have a good seating position (it's often best to be next to the person who is in the chair) with a clear view of all the participants.

Learn effective note-taking

However senior you are, you'll probably find yourself acting as note-taker at some meetings. It's impossible to write as quickly as you can speak so just concentrate on capturing the key points.

Here are two simple tips for note-taking:

1. Develop your own personal shorthand – not Pitman's, just a rough and ready way of getting things down on paper as quickly as you can. You can often do this by abbreviating words, omitting vowels or just writing initials. As long as you yourself know what the shortened word or initials stand for, that's all that matters. You might want to use some of the abbreviations used in text messaging.

2. Watch out for key words and signals. If someone says "I'm going to make three main points" or "to sum up..." the note-taker should be on red alert. It's especially important to watch out for—and to record clearly and accurately— key points, conclusions, decisions, recommendations and action points.

Top tips for effective meetings

Here are my top tips for contributing effectively to meetings:

- Read the papers and get to grips with the subject-matter.
- Be clear about your objective.
- Write yourself a brief speaking note.
- Secure a good seating position.
- Look alert and ready to contribute.
- Maintain eye contact.
- Speak with energy and conviction – and not too fast.
- Build on others' contributions.
- Label your interventions ("I would like to make two points...").
- Speak clearly and succinctly.
- Be positive and constructive (if you have to say No to something, suggest an alternative to which you might be able to say Yes).
- Generate light, not heat – stay calm and don't lose your temper.
- Take your own notes of key comments/points (even when there is an official note-taker).

What makes a bad meeting?

It's easy to have a bad meeting. Here are some examples:

- No clear purpose.
- Goes on too long.
- No agenda or papers.
- Chair has no real grasp of subject-matter.
- Chair has no control.
- Chair is domineering or insensitive.
- Dominated by one or two people.
- Attended by the wrong people.
- Participants have not prepared or read the papers.
- No introductions: no-one knows who the other people are and which organisations they represent.
- Participants arrive late.
- Chair does not clarify or summarise.
- Participants only interested in pushing their own views – not prepared to listen.
- Poor logistics (e.g. room, seating, heating/ventilation, refreshments, technical aids, interruptions, etc).
- Nothing agreed – no clear outcome.
- Nobody knows what will happen next.

Keep it short

Most meetings go on too long! It's good practice to set a firm time-limit at the outset. The optimum length obviously depends upon the amount and complexity of the business to be discussed. But for many meetings 30 minutes or an hour is an adequate and realistic timeframe. If there is an agenda with several items of business, it's often useful to designate a time-limit for each item. Put the most urgent and important items near the top of the agenda – just in case, despite your best efforts, you do not succeed in getting through the whole agenda in the time available.

Stay awake

If the business is so important or so difficult to deal with that a long meeting is inescapable, both the person chairing the meeting and the other participants will need to make a conscious effort to maintain concentration. Listening is hard work. Absorbing information and getting to grips with the key points requires a conscious effort, especially if the speaker just drones on and on, without making much effort to interest the listeners.

It's very easy to let your attention wander; to think about more interesting things, such as the novel you're reading or the holiday you're planning. Put all those pleasant thoughts to the back of your mind. Look at whoever is speaking and concentrate on what he/she is saying. It might be boring, but it's what you're being paid to do.

Participants must prepare too

Anyone participating in a meeting needs to prepare if they are to make a useful contribution. Read the relevant papers and get to grips with the subject matter. If this is difficult or contentious you'll probably need to sound out the views of others in advance of the meeting. You'll need to be clear about what you want to get out of the meeting. Then you can plan your contribution and write yourself a brief speaking note.

Chapter summary

- Make sure you really do need to have a meeting.

- Be crystal clear about the purpose.

- Prepare thoroughly, and get the papers out in good time.

- Be polite and courteous but firm and businesslike.

- Help people to feel comfortable.

- Use your interpersonal skills to encourage contributions – and to discourage over-long or irrelevant interventions.

- Make sure the logistics run like clockwork.

- It's the chair's job to summarise, clarify and question.

- Make sure you have an accurate record of the meeting, even if it's simply a note of agreed action points.

The conventional definition of management is getting work done through people, but real management is developing people through work.

Agha Hasan Abedi

Managing projects
It's not rocket science

chapter 5
Managing projects

The need to manage projects is nothing new – just think of the Victorians' great civil engineering works. Project management as a recognised discipline dates from the mid-1950s. Initially used for major construction and energy projects, its use has spread to virtually every type of activity. Today any manager at any level is likely to find himself/herself managing a project of some kind.

Project management has become a subject studied in centres of learning all over the world. It has given rise to an enormous body of literature and countless methodologies, many of them seemingly impenetrable to anyone who has not been to a top business school.

Yet project management is not rocket science. In fact, it's very simple. It boils down to just three things:

- Being clear about the end-result – the outcome you're seeking to achieve.
- Identifying the steps you need to take in order to achieve that outcome.
- Putting mechanisms in place to ensure that you these steps are taken and that the project is completed on time, within budget and to the required standard.

Anyone (well, almost anyone!) can become a competent project manager.

How to define a project

Projects come in all shapes and sizes, from organising a media event (perhaps to launch a new product or announce a new initiative) to developing a multi-million pound computer network. Most definitions of a project have two key characteristics: a clearly defined timescale within which it must be completed; and clearly defined resources with which to carry it out.

Be clear about the purpose of the project

The first essential is to be crystal clear about the purpose of your project. What is the outcome you are seeking to achieve? This may have been defined by your boss or your top management team. Or you may need to define it for yourself. Think about the project's added value and the difference it will make to the organisation. Define the desired outcome as clearly and precisely as you can.

Get buy-in from your stakeholders

Any major project needs to be supported by the key stakeholders. This is critically important. If you don't have their support, the chances are that, sooner or later, you'll hit trouble. So take care to identify the key people. Cast your net as widely as you can, both within your organisation and beyond, and make a list of them. Then go down the list and annotate it from two different perspectives: first, how much power or influence the stakeholder has in relation to the project; secondly, how much interest he/she has in it. This will enable you to put each stakeholder into one of four categories:

- if they have a lot of power and a lot of interest in the project, try to **involve** them;
- if they have a lot of power but not much interest in the project, keep them **informed** about it;
- if they have a lot of interest in the project but little or no power, **listen** to them;
- if they have neither power nor interest in the project, you can probably **ignore** them.

Review your stakeholders periodically

Stakeholders change. Some will disappear from your radar screen and new ones will appear. And the amount of power they have, or the amount of interest they have in your project, may change. So keep an eye on them, especially in the case of a major project taking months or years to complete. Periodically review your list of stakeholders and the extent to which you need to involve or inform them. From time to time you'll need to make some changes.

Keep key stakeholders in the picture

There are plenty of reasons why it's a good idea to keep your key stakeholders involved or informed – especially in the case of a major project with far-reaching implications. It helps to gain their commitment and co-operation. It helps to guard against unrealistic expectations. It gives them an improved understanding of the issues and problems involved in implementing the project. And it can help to avoid unpleasant surprises – both for the stakeholders and for the project manager!

Identify the risks and the obstacles

Once you're clear about the purpose of the project and the desired outcome, and you have identified your key stakeholders, the next step is to think about all the things that could go wrong. If it's a big project, there will be lots of them; but even if your project is the production of a simple report or a sales leaflet, there are bound to be some things that could prevent its successful completion. You need to identify the risks and potential obstacles. Brainstorming (see Chapter 9) can be a useful technique for this.

Consider the probability and the impact

Once you have identified all the risks and obstacles, you need to ask, in respect of each one, two important questions. First, how probable is it that this will materialise? Secondly, if it does materialise, what will the impact be? If something would have a huge impact on the project (say, an earthquake) but is extremely improbable, you can ignore it. Equally, if something is very probable (say, a member of your team leaving to take up a new job) but would have little or no impact on the project, that too can be ignored.

Rank the risks and obstacles

A simple and easy way of ranking both for probability and for impact is to give each risk and obstacle one of five rankings: very high, high, medium, low, very low. If you then put this information onto a graph or spreadsheet you'll be able to see at a glance the probability and the impact of each risk and obstacle.

" The real problem
is what to do with
problem solvers after
the problem is solved.

Gay Talese

Now you can focus your attention on those which are most probable and will have most impact on the project. For example, you might decide to concentrate just on those which come out with at least a high ranking both for probability and for impact.

Deal with the risks and obstacles

Once you have identified those things likely to materialise which will have a significant impact, you need to decide what, if anything, you can do about them. There are four main possibilities:

- prevention: action to stop the risk arising or to remove the obstacle;
- reduction: action to reduce the probability or to limit the impact;
- contingency: action that can be taken if the risk or obstacle does materialise;
- acceptance: simply accept that no action is feasible.

In an extreme case, where significant risks or obstacles which will have a high impact on the project are very likely to materialise, and where nothing can be done about these, it may be necessary to abort the project. In practice it is almost always possible to find some way of at least reducing the probability or limiting the impact. What is important is that those involved in planning and implementing the project are aware of the potential risks and obstacles – and of the action that can be taken if they materialise.

Break the project down into manageable chunks

The next step is to break the project down into manageable chunks of work. You can approach this task from two angles: what you put into the project, and what you get out of it. It's usually best to begin by defining what you want to get out of the project – the outputs.

Don't confuse your outputs with your outcome

Do you know the difference between an outcome and an output? The outcome is the end result you want to achieve. Outputs are the result of the work you do – the specific things or products that the project will deliver. It's essential to ensure that the outputs really do contribute to the desired outcome.

Make sure your outputs are SMART

- **S**pecific
- **M**easurable
- **A**greed
- **R**ealistic
- **T**ime-limited

It's important that outputs are defined as precisely as possible: the more specific they are, the easier they are to measure. They need to be realistic and to be agreed with key stakeholders.

Don't be confused by the terms

It's easy to be confused by some of the terminology used in project management. The same words are sometimes used in different ways. Some organisations, for example, think of outputs in terms of activities.

Some organisations have targets (rather than outputs) for absolutely everything, while others limit targets to a small number of key outputs. A manager may have, say, a dozen outputs which he/she is responsible for delivering. But if two or three of these outputs are critical to the organisation's success, these may be expressed as specific, quantifiable targets which he/she is expected to hit (or to exceed) within a specified timescale.

Words such as aims, goals and objectives can also cause confusion, not least because management gurus tend to define these in slightly different ways. The aim or goal is the end-result you want to achieve. So both these words are really just alternatives for outcome. An objective is usually something intermediate which you need to achieve in order to end up with your desired outcome.

Don't get too hung up on any one definition of any of these words. What's important is to understand the (essentially simple) steps and processes involved.

Plan your project

These are the steps you can take to plan your project:

- Be clear about the end-result (the outcome) you are seeking to achieve.

- Define the specific outputs (and/or targets) that will enable you to achieve the desired outcome.

- Agree the timeframe.

- Clarify what resources (human and financial) are available.

- Draw up a list of the activities that need to be undertaken in order to produce each of the specified outputs. Think carefully about linkages and dependencies – the order in which activities are carried out. Some can be carried out in parallel, whereas some will be dependent upon the completion of other activities. It's good practice to assign responsibility for each activity to one named individual.

Use a Gannt chart to plan your activities

A Gannt chart is a horizontal bar chart widely used in project management to plan, co-ordinate and track specific tasks. It was originally developed in 1917 by Henry L. Gantt, an American engineer and social scientist, as a production control tool.

A Gannt chart is useful for planning activities over a period of time. Here is a very simple example. Obviously, the timeframe and the units of time allocated to each activity depend on the nature and the complexity of the project.

	January	February	March	April	May
Activity A	███				
Activity B		███			
Activity C	███				
Activity D			███	███	
Activity E					███

Use milestones and performance criteria

How do you know whether or not you're on track to complete your project on time, within budget and to the required standard? The answer is to establish performance criteria and milestones – specific points throughout the implementation period when you will monitor how things are going.

For each milestone, specify exactly how much progress should have been made (e.g. outputs, budget utilisation, performance criteria to be met). It's important to establish performance criteria which are relevant and appropriate for whatever it is that you are seeking to measure. They may include such things as statistical comparisons, quality checks, regular reports and audits.

Once you've established milestones and performance criteria, you'll be in a position to compare actual performance with planned performance. You'll know whether or not you're on schedule. If you are, fine. If you're behind schedule, consider what action you can take to get the project back on track. If you're ahead of schedule (it can happen!), go out and celebrate.

Consider using project management software

Software programmes (such as Microsoft Project) can be useful to help plan and monitor a project. These typically include Gannt charts and some of the other tools mentioned in this chapter. Some people like these programmes and some don't, but it's probably worthwhile taking a look at what is available.

Don't keep it all to yourself

Communication is a vital part of any project manager's job. Whether your project is going well or not, it's important to keep your major stakeholders, in particular, informed of progress. If you don't, you'll only store up trouble.

Be on time

Many projects are time-critical. If your project includes the launch of a new product at a conference scheduled for 1 March, you won't be popular if your publicity material for the launch is not ready until 2 March. If being excellent means being late, it is usually better to be a little less excellent but on time.

Put it into practice

You're now equipped to put all this stuff into practice. You're clear about the desired outcome and the outputs you have to deliver in order to achieve it. You know who your stakeholders are, what the likely risks and obstacles are, and how you'll handle them. You know how much time you have and what resources are available. You know what needs to be done and who is going to do it. You have everything you need to be a brilliant project manager!

Chapter summary

- Be clear about the desired outcome of your project.

- Identify and involve key stakeholders.

- Identify risks and obstacles, and assess their probability and potential impact.

- Consider what action you can take to deal with any risks that materialise.

- Break the project down into manageable chunks of work.

- Set yourself outputs which are specific, measurable, agreed, realistic and time-limited.

- Agree the timeframe and the resources available.

- Plan the activities to be undertaken in order to produce your outputs, and assign responsibility for each one to a named individual.

- Establish milestones and performance criteria to enable you to keep track of progress.

- Make sure you complete the project on time, within budget and to the required standard.

"Leadership means making people feel good.

Jean Chrétien

Managing communication
Keep it short and simple

chapter 6
Managing communication

Probably no other aspect of management has changed as radically and rapidly as communication. Twenty years ago I used to dictate my letters, reports, minutes and memos to a shorthand typist, or write them out in longhand and pass them to the typing pool. Then PCs and faxes came in. Now we have emails and the Internet, and it's difficult to imagine how I ever managed without a laptop or a mobile phone.

The technology has moved on, but the essentials of effective communication are the same as ever:

- Be crystal clear about the message you're seeking to communicate.

- Identify the target audience as precisely as you can, and put yourself in the shoes of the person(s) or the organisation you're communicating with.

- Put the message across as clearly, simply and succinctly as you can.

Quite often problems within any organisation can be traced back to a breakdown in communication. Successful organisations recognise this and make effective communication a key priority.

Every manager needs communication skills, and the more senior you are, the more important they become.

Make sure you understand the message

You can't communicate effectively if you don't understand—really understand—the message you're seeking to put across. So the first, crucial step is to take time to brief yourself thoroughly. Whatever the subject-matter, whatever the audience, you won't be listened to with respect unless you can show that you know what you're talking about. Get to grips with the subject and make sure you've got the essential facts at your fingertips.

Keep it short and simple (KISS)

Ask the first person you meet in a strange town for directions, or listen to any radio chat show, and you'll realise that many people have difficulty expressing themselves simply and clearly. If you want to communicate effectively, clarity and brevity are essential.

KISS (Keep It Short and Simple) is the easiest of acronyms to remember. The longer and more complex the message, the less likely it is to be remembered. Politicians and public relations people know this. That's why, day in, day out, they use catchy slogans and short, snappy sound-bites. They know it works.

Put yourself in their shoes

Try to put yourself in the shoes of the person or the organisation you're communicating with. Think about how much they already know about the subject and how much interest they have in it. Consider what concerns they will have and how they are likely to react. This will give you some clues about how you can put the message across most effectively.

Tell the truth

It's important to give everyone the same message – even if it's likely to be unpalatable to some people. If you give different people a different message, you'll get a reputation for unreliability and double-dealing. It might enable you to deal more easily with the immediate issue, but it will damage your credibility and do you no good in the long run.

…But tell it differently

On the other hand, it's sensible to adjust the way you put the message across —the facts and the arguments you use to support it—in order to make it as acceptable as you can to the individual or the organisation you're dealing with. Make sure the essential message is the same, but tweak the way you deliver it. Just choose those facts and arguments that are most relevant and are most likely to go down well. Of course, the better you know your target audience (the more you understand where they are coming from) the easier this is.

Circumstances alter cases

How you communicate will be affected to some extent by the culture of your organisation—"the way things are done around here"—as well as by your own personal style. But most of all, it should be dictated by the particular circumstances – what exactly it is you have to communicate, how important that is, and to whom you have to communicate it. You have to use your experience and your common sense.

Think about how to communicate with your team

If you have something to communicate to your team, take a second to think about how you're going to do it. You could call a meeting. You could bash out an email. You could put the information into a memo and send that out, either as hard copy or as an attachment to an email. You could speak to people on the telephone. You could pass the information on to just one other person (perhaps your deputy, if you have one) and ask him/her to pass it on to the rest of the team. You could ask people to come to see you individually at your desk. Or you could visit each member of your team at his/her desk. There are lots of possibilities. Decide which is the most appropriate and effective way to communicate that particular piece of information.

Communicate with energy and confidence

Whatever it is you have to communicate, do it with enthusiasm. Diffidence or hesitancy can undermine the most brilliant message. On the other hand, even a weak message can convince if it's put across with energy, conviction and confidence. Ask any politician.

Don't overdo it

Having too much information is just as bad as having too little. If you're inundated with lots of inconsequential emails, it's quite likely that you'll overlook the one that is really urgent and important. Don't bombard your staff or your colleagues with stuff they don't need to see.

" I can live for two
months on one
good compliment. "

Mark Twain

Don't waffle, but adjust your approach to suit the context

If you speak at great length without saying anything much, people will soon lose interest and switch off. So don't waffle and beat about the bush.

How to put across the message most effectively depends both on the context and the subject-matter. Sometimes it's best to come right out with a succinct statement of your conclusion, and then to back this up with the facts and the arguments.

Sometimes—especially if others are unlikely to agree with your opinion or your conclusion—it is better to take your audience by the hand and lead up, step by step, to the conclusion. Use whichever tactics are most appropriate and most likely to succeed, bearing in mind both the subject-matter and the person(s) you're communicating with.

Communication is a two-way process

Communication is not just about giving out information. If you're communicating orally, you need to give those you're communicating with an opportunity to react. This helps to ensure that the message has been received and understood. It's important to give people an opportunity to express their views and to ask questions. Whether the reaction is positive or negative (or something in between), you need this feedback.

With written communication, too, it's usually a good idea to make it easy for the recipient(s) to provide feedback. You can often do this simply by including your contact details, such as an email address.

Written communication needs to be clear and concise

As a general principle, write in a style that's as close as you can make it to the way you speak. That doesn't mean using slang or colloquialisms that would look ugly on a printed page. It just means using plain English: direct, everyday language.

The English language has two main derivations, Latin and Anglo-Saxon. Latin, which has not been spoken since the Middle Ages, became associated with learning, while Anglo-Saxon was regarded as the commoners' language. This distinction is kept up today by a few writers who hope to impress their readers by using unfamiliar words and a flowery style of writing.

Usually the word derived from Anglo-Saxon is shorter (and often more concrete) than the Latinate equivalent – for example, begin, rather than commence; end, rather than terminate; light, rather than illuminate. If there is a short word that will do the job, choose that in preference to a longer alternative.

Use short sentences (as I do in *The Greatest Management Tips in the World*). They are easier to read than longer sentences with complicated constructions and lots of subsidiary clauses. Between 15 and 20 words is a good average.

Finally, use short paragraphs. A page of solid text, or one page split into just two huge paragraphs, does not invite you to read it. Short paragraphs are easier on the eye.

Long words . . .versus. . . short words

Ascertain	find out
Assist	help
Commence	begin
Component	part
Concept	idea
Concerning	about
Demonstrate	show
Discontinue	stop, end
Endeavour	try, attempt
Establish	set up, form
Forward	send
Illuminate	light
Initiate	start
Necessitate	require, need
Permit	let
Principal	main
Provide	give
Purchase	buy
Regarding	about
Terminate	end

Pay attention to presentation

Written communication also needs to be clearly presented. That means using plenty of white space – decent margins and paragraph breaks. Use headings and sub-headings in bold to make it easy for readers to find their way through. Take care over the font type and size, making sure that it's appropriate for the purpose and easy to read. If you have a small number of key points to put across, use bullets to make them stand out.

Before you send it out, check it

However much care you take over the text, it's very easy to make simple mistakes or typos. Once you have sent it out, it's too late to do anything about it. If the text has gone out with some ghastly mistake and you have to issue a subsequent correction, that won't do your professional reputation any good. So check the text meticulously before you send it out.

Look especially carefully at names (people can get very annoyed it you misspell them), titles, initials denoting honours or academic qualifications, and numbers. These are all things it's very easy to slip up on. It's also a good idea to get a colleague to cast any eye over it. If you are very close to a subject it is sometimes difficult to spot errors: you might read what is in your mind rather than what is on the page. A colleague who is less closely involved with the substance of the communication may pick up typos or other little mistakes that you have missed.

Put it away for a day

When you have finished writing anything, it's always a good idea to put it way for a day or so and then to look at it again with fresh eyes. As a writer I know that the final text is always better than the first draft. If you put it away and come back to it later, you'll be able to look at it more objectively. Invariably you'll spot something you can improve: perhaps a sentence you don't need, or a word that's not quite the right one, or something important that you've omitted, or just something that can be said more clearly and more concisely. Give it a try!

Obviously, when you're up against a tight deadline, this may not be possible. If that's the case, at least get a member of your team to cast an eye over it before you send it out.

Make emails work for you

Emails are wonderful. With a few taps on the keyboard you can send your message anywhere in the world. It's quick and easy. It enables you to send out all kinds of documents without going to the trouble and expense of printing and posting out hard copies. Whatever business your organisation is in, emails are an indispensable aid to handling work effectively and efficiently.

Because emails are so quick and easy to send and to receive, there's a tendency to over-use them. Sometimes, because of the nature of the document or its confidentiality, a hard copy really is essential. And sometimes nothing but a one-to-one conversation, either face to face or on the phone, will do. So before you hit the send button, just take a moment or two to consider whether an email really is the best option.

Is this what they really mean?

- Ball park figure – a figure that has as much chance of being accurate as I have of winning the national lottery.

- Blue skies thinking – I'll contribute some theoretical, totally impractical ideas. I'm much too important to worry about the detail.

- By close of play – a beautifully vague timeframe which can be interpreted to mean anything from 4 p.m. to midnight.

- Co-ordination – a means of either duplicating or counteracting what others elsewhere in the organisation are doing.

- For information – don't even think about commenting on this. But if it goes wrong, I won't forget that you knew all about it.

- Happy to discuss – there's a lot more going on here than meets the eye. I haven't told you the half of it.

- In due course – in a very long time (if I remember).

- I'd welcome your thoughts – I haven't the foggiest notion what this is about. Can you help me out? Then I can pinch your ideas and take all the credit.

- I have taken careful note of your suggestion – your suggestion was rubbish and it's gone straight into the waste paper basket.

- I hope this is helpful – I know very well that this is not at all helpful. Please go away and don't bother me again.

- Please deal – you can do the work on this: it's either too boring or too difficult for me.

- Review – something is going wrong, but we can't admit it.

- Stakeholders – all those people who know nothing about the organisation and care even less.

- Strategy – a word which makes people think you know which direction the organisation is going in, when neither you nor anyone else has a clue.

- Target audience – the poor sods who have to put up with all the guff the organisation puts out.

- The points you have made will be taken into account – your points were ridiculous and irrelevant, and will be ignored.

- Toolkit – implies you're approaching an issue methodically and have a range of problem-solving techniques, when in reality you're groping around in the dark.

- Work/life balance – I'm the boss here and I'm going home early. You can stay behind and work late.

- You will recall – I didn't either until I dug out the old papers.

- You will wish to be aware – No, you won't. I'm afraid it's very bad news.

Don't let emails rule your life

It's very easy to waste time constantly checking your inbox or reading and responding to inconsequential emails that are much easier to deal with than the piece of work you should really be tackling. It's a good idea to reserve one or two specific time slots during the day for dealing with emails, perhaps first thing in the morning and last thing in the evening. If an email needs a reply, try to send it the same day.

Take a note

I've already suggested taking your own brief note of any meeting you attend. The same goes for one-to-one discussions and important phone conversations. You'll be surprised how useful this can turn out to be.

Keep a copy

Keep a copy of every email, memo, report and any other communication you send out. With computer storage now so vast, it's easy to do. You're sure to need to check back.

Avoid jargon

All organisations use jargon, and that's fine – provided everyone involved understands it. But if you're communicating with the outside world, it's vital to avoid jargon, acronyms and, indeed, any terms with which the recipient is unfamiliar. You need to make sure that every word you use is comprehensible. If you use jargon to communicate with the outside world, you might just as well use a foreign language.

Use websites and the Internet sensibly

A well-designed website, which both customers and the public at large can find their way around quickly and easily, is something that no organisation can now afford to be without.

Thanks to the Internet it's possible to obtain instant information about anything under the sun. Use it sensibly. It's easy to waste an enormous amount of time surfing the net and looking at all kinds of stuff that's absolutely fascinating —but not at all relevant to the job you are being paid to do.

Chapter summary

- Keep communication as short and simple as you can.
- Be clear about the message you're seeking to put across.
- Put yourself in the shoes of the person(s) or organisation you're communicating with.
- Tell the truth and give everyone the same message, but adjust the way you put it across to make it acceptable.
- Remember that communication is a two way process: you need to listen as well as to tell.
- If you're writing, use plain language and short sentences.
- Keep paragraphs short; use headings and sub-headings and have plenty of white space.
- When you've finished writing, put it away for a day or so and then look at it again with fresh eyes.
- Use emails sensibly.

"A leader is most effective when people barely know he exists. When his work is done, his aim fulfilled, his troops will feel they did it themselves.

Hippocrates 460 BC-380 BC

Managing teams

More than a bunch of people who work together

chapter 7
Managing teams

The days of autocratic bosses and employees who just do as they are told are pretty much over. No organisation can hope to survive today unless it makes the best possible use of its human resources. That means using the experience, knowledge and skills of its entire people. Every one of them has individual strengths (as well as weaknesses), and team-working is the way to make the most of them. An effective team adds value because it contributes more than the sum of its individual components.

Of course, not all organisations have fully embraced team working. Lecturers and training consultants, for example, are often strongly individualistic and like to do their own thing in their own way. Yet even here there is room for an element of team working. A university lecturer needs to work with administrative support staff, and will almost certainly improve the quality of lectures by sharing ideas, experience and expertise with colleagues working in the same field.

Not long ago I used to captain a village cricket team. I tried to give every player an opportunity to show what he could (or, as it turned out in most cases, could not) do. I tried to "walk the talk", not so much by my (less than scintillating) batting as by showing enthusiasm, commitment, determination and good humour. Occasionally I have felt that, compared to a village cricket team, managing a team at work is a doddle!

Be clear about it: what is a team?

Let's begin by defining what we mean by a team. There's no one definition accepted by all the experts. For my money the essential characteristics of a team are: a clearly defined membership; a role that is understood and accepted throughout the organisation; clear aims and objectives; and continuous collaboration and interdependency which enable the team to achieve goals that individuals alone could not achieve. We can turn this into a one-sentence working definition: "a group of people, with complementary skills, experience and roles, who work together to achieve common and agreed aims."

Recognise the stages of team development

Probably the most widely accepted model of team development is B. W. Tuckman's (published in 1965 in Psychological Bulletin 63, pp 384-399). He saw team development in four stages:

- Forming: members of the team come together, get to know one another, explore their strengths and weaknesses, and win each other's respect;
- Storming: attitudinal and temperamental differences emerge and are discussed and debated;
- Norming: the team settles down and works out ways of working effectively together;
- Performing: the team, having dealt with its internal problems, gets stuck into its work and achieves its goals.

A team is not a collection of individuals

A team is a unit with its own distinctive qualities, conventions and dynamics. "We're in this together" is the phrase that epitomises the team mentality.

Put a team together – or make the best of what you've got

Occasionally you may find yourself in the happy position of setting up a team from scratch. You'll probably find that resources are limited and that you'll have to settle for less than you would ideally like. Putting a team together can be exciting: you'll probably need to use all your interpersonal skills to get them all on board!

More often, you'll have to work with the team you're given. Your job as a manager is to make the best possible use of the resources you've got. That means using the individual skills and knowledge of each member of your team to maximum effect.

Define the team's role

The team's role needs to be crystal clear. Everyone needs to understand exactly what its remit is, where it sits in the organisational structure, and to whom it is responsible. You'll need to consider how its work will affect, or be affected by, what others elsewhere in the organisation are doing; to avoid any duplication or overlap; and to ensure that others take account of the team's activities. If there is any likelihood of demarcation disputes, it's best to get these sorted out at the outset.

Team characteristics

- A clear identity with clear objectives.
- Clarity about roles and responsibilities.
- Accountability as a team.
- Keeping one another fully informed.
- Honesty and openness.
- Shared rewards.
- Helping one another to develop.
- Acceptance of common rules and discipline.
- Mutual support.
- Sharing professional knowledge.
- Learning from other team members.
- Making the best use of complementary skills and experience.
- Pooling ideas and using the best.
- Sharing problems.
- Bouncing ideas off people who speak the same language.
- Respect for other team members.
- Trusting other team members.
- Common goals.
- Its own culture.
- "We" mentality.
- Shared values.
- Common standards of performance.

Be clear about the team's objectives

It's vital that every member of the team has a clear understanding both of the team's objectives and of what he/she personally is expected to contribute. Begin by establishing team outputs which are SMART (specific, measurable, agreed, realistic and time-limited). The clearer and more specific these are, the better, and the easier it will be to monitor and evaluate the team's performance.

Identify the skills and experience

If you're setting up a team from scratch, consider what experience and skills you'll need. Go through each of the team's objectives in turn: think about the main tasks that will have to be undertaken, and identify the specific competencies needed. If that sounds easy enough, don't be fooled. You'll probably find that you have some of the necessary experience and skills in abundance – alongside some gaping holes.

If resources are limited (and they will be) you'll have to make some compromises. For example, you might decide to exclude someone who has first-rate technical skills, on the grounds that someone else has adequate technical skills alongside other attributes (such as strong interpersonal skills) which will be of greater overall benefit to the team.

If you can't get all the skills you need within the team itself, you may have to settle for obtaining some of them from outside as and when you need them.

See who can play which team role(s)

The work of Dr Meredith Belbin has identified nine team roles, each with its strengths and weaknesses. Importantly, Belbin recognises that most people have more than one preferred team role: typically they have three or four roles which they can adopt as the situation requires. Some of the key characteristics covered by the nine roles described in Belbin's model are:

- Creative and imaginative.
- Enthusiastic and communicative.
- Goals-orientated and decision-focussed.
- Dynamic and determined.
- Strategic and capable of accurate judgement.
- Co-operative and team-orientated.
- Disciplined and practical.
- Painstaking and conscientious.
- Having specialist knowledge and skills.

Use analytical psychology to define personality traits

Carl Jung, a Swiss psychiatrist who developed a unique system of analytical psychology, observed that people relate to the world in four different ways: intellectually, emotionally, imaginatively and physically.

Jung's observation can be translated into broad personality traits along the following lines:

- (the capability to) approach problems logically and objectively;
- take account of the human dimension and the way people feel;
- come up with imaginative solutions;
- promote those solutions to the outside world.

A team needs all these four capabilities. If you're the team leader, make sure that you have each of these dimensions covered by at least one member.

Examine your own style preferences – and think about those of others

Jung's work has led to the development of personality profiling models (one of the best known is Myers Briggs) to help people understand differences in working styles. It's important to recognise that these models are non-judgemental: they describe working preferences – not skills or abilities. They reflect normal differences between healthy people! Here are some examples:

- If you have an extrovert style, you'll prefer to develop ideas through discussion, talk through problems, speak or act first and reflect later, and communicate orally. With an introvert style, you'll prefer to develop ideas internally and think through problems, focus on the task and work without interruption, reflect before speaking, and communicate in writing.

- In dealing with information, you'll either (a) collect specific facts and evidence before reaching a conclusion, and have a practical, realistic approach to problems, or (b) prefer to focus on the big picture, and be interested in ideas and new challenges.

- In making decisions, you'll either (a) weigh up the evidence logically, apply consistent principles and reach an objective conclusion, or (b) decide issues on the basis of your own values and beliefs, and try to accommodate others and reach consensus.

- In managing yourself and your work, you'll either (a) be methodical and organised, enjoy decision-making and like to get things settled quickly, or (b) feel restricted by schedules and timescales, like to be spontaneous, and prefer to keep your options open.

Be sceptical

Human beings are complicated creatures. Most people have a mixture of personality traits and working styles, and do not fit neatly into little boxes. So be a little sceptical about all this stuff. However, Belbin's team role theory, Jung's work and models based on it can help you to:

- understand yourself and your own behaviour better;

- appreciate the impact of your behaviour on others;

- adapt your working style to accommodate others;

- see that it can be useful to approach issues in different ways.

Appraising individual performance

Most organisations have a system for appraising individual performance at least once a year. The detailed procedures vary, but we can identify some key principles:

- Provide continuous feedback: the annual appraisal should not come as a nasty shock! If someone has made a bad mistake or produced poor work, it is best if the manager points this out immediately – not for the purpose of apportioning blame, but in order to get the individual to recognise that something has gone wrong and to help him/her to ensure that it does not happen again. Similarly, if someone has produced an excellent piece of work, congratulate him/her immediately. When you give feedback, avoid generalities: it's very important to be specific and factual. Whether the feedback is positive or negative, substantiate it by giving concrete examples.

- Seek input from the job holder: the person doing the job knows more about it than anyone else! Involving the job holder in the process gives him/her some control over his/her work – a key factor in obtaining commitment.

- Attack the problem, not the person: objective identification of problems and rational discussion (both of the facts and of possible solutions) should help both the manager and the job holder to address issues constructively and to arrive at an agreed solution.

- Prepare thoroughly for the appraisal meeting: both manager and job holder need to assemble facts and evidence to support their view of performance achieved during the past year, and to think about tasks and objectives for the year ahead. The discussion itself should have four phases:

1. Review what has been achieved during the past year and compare this with the tasks and objectives agreed at the beginning of the year.

2. Identify and explore factors, both internal and external, which have affected performance (for good or bad). Don't let this become antagonistic or recriminatory: the manager's key skills here are questioning and active listening.

3. Agree new tasks and objectives: it is usually best if these are proposed by the job holder. They can then be discussed and changed as necessary in order to agree a list which meets the needs both of the manager and of the job holder.

4. Identify training and development needs: it is often useful to divide these into short-term (training) requirements, to help the individual improve performance in the current job, and longer term needs related to future career development.

Tasks and objectives should be:

- linked to organisational objectives
- listed in priority order
- specific
- measurable (quantity and time are often the most useful measures)
- challenging but realistic

360 degree appraisal can be useful

This form of appraisal involves receiving feedback on performance not only from the individual's manager, but also from subordinates, colleagues at the same level, and others for whom work is done or to whom a service is provided. 360 degree feedback is being introduced in an increasing number of organisations, particularly at senior levels. It tends to give the job holder a pretty accurate idea of how he/she is perceived, but it needs to be handled extremely carefully and sensitively. It is usual for the feedback to be filtered for confidentiality, so that the job holder cannot identify the comments of specific individuals, and to be channelled through a third party.

Lead by example

If you're the team leader, the very best way to lead is by example: "walk the talk", as the Americans say. You need to model, and to put into practice on a daily basis, those standards which you are seeking to instil into others. Setting a good example is such an obvious principle of leadership that it should hardly need saying. Yet I have known one or two very senior people for whom the proverb "do as I say, not as I do" might have been invented!

Show leadership

What do we mean by leadership? As with management, there are lots of different definitions. To my mind one of the best is "getting people to do something because they want to." It's probably easier, however, to identify what we expect of a leader.

For my money a leader needs:

- to have vision;
- to give purpose and direction;
- to lead by example – "walk the talk";
- to inspire and motivate – to get the best out of people;
- to involve people in matters that affect them before final decisions are taken;
- to think strategically and set clear objectives;
- to seek continuous improvement;
- to home in on key principles and issues;
- to act honestly and even-handedly;
- to be visible and approachable;
- to communicate clearly and persuasively;
- to have energy and enthusiasm;
- to be resilient and tough under pressure.

Remember that every manager is a leader

Many management gurus make a clear distinction between leadership and management. I'm not altogether comfortable with that. Obviously, if you're at the top of an organisation, it's vital to have a clear vision of the future, and to know where the organisation is going and how it's going to get there. But a key component of leadership—to my mind, the most important of all—is the ability to motivate people. And that is something that every manager, however junior, needs – even if he/she is responsible for managing just one member of staff.

"We started off trying to set up a small anarchist community, but people wouldn't obey the rules.

Alan Bennett

Be a team player

Are you a team player? Not just someone who goes through the motions? It's not unknown for people to pay lip-service to team-working while taking every opportunity to promote their own personal interests at the expense of the team. If the team is to be an effective force, all team members need to pull in the same direction. If one person bad-mouths the team, its leader or other team members to people outside the team, that's bound to reflect badly on the whole team. If it continues for any length of time, morale will suffer. If you're in a team, it's your duty to support, promote and even fight for the team.

Don't wash dirty linen in public – but wash it

No team is perfect. You may well have gripes about the way the team or its leader operates, or about the way a particular issue or a particular project is being handled. Don't be tempted to give vent to your feelings in front of an outside audience. Being a member of a team is a bit like being in the Cabinet!

You can have all the arguments and disagreements you like within the team. But once you're facing the outside world, it's your duty to present a common front. On the other hand, if you're unhappy about the way things are being done or if something is going seriously wrong, don't hesitate to speak up about it within the team. Try to do this in a constructive way: if something isn't working, suggest an alternative that you believe would work.

Treat the team as if it were your family

Families are not always harmonious, but one of the characteristics of stable, enduring family relationships is a willingness to support and protect other family members against the outside world. Mutual support, help and protection is an important characteristic of successful teams. If someone else in the team is under pressure, try to help out. You might need some help yourself one day.

Don't keep it to yourself

Information is power! That does not mean that you should keep it all to yourself. If you don't share what you know with those around you, they're unlikely to share what they know with you. Everyone should know, at least in general terms, what projects or tasks others are working on. If one person picks up an important piece of news, it should be shared with the rest of the team. Then, if that person is suddenly taken ill, the information won't be lost to the rest of the world. A brief email can be a good way of passing on information, especially if members of the team spend a lot of time away from the office.

Be flexible - know what works for whom

We're all different: the way we work, the way we think, the way we relate to those around us, the way we respond to praise or criticism, the way we cope with the unexpected. Some people respond well to pressure, and thrive when faced with a challenging deadline. Others need lots of praise and encouragement to produce their best work. Yet others need a firm framework, and respond better to a stick than a carrot.

Remember that your team is a collection of individuals, all with different personalities, different strengths and weaknesses – and different foibles. As their manager, it's your job to get to know what makes each of them tick.

Delegate!

Delegation enables you to make maximum use of your resources. It also helps the team to gain new experience and new skills, and to grow and develop. I have led different teams in different parts of the world doing very different types of work. The contexts and the culture—and the personalities of team members—could hardly have been more different, but in all of them delegation enabled me to make effective use of whatever skills and knowledge each individual had.

...But delegate carefully

If you decide to delegate a piece of work, don't just give it to whoever happens to be passing by. Give the matter a little thought. Think about what that task will involve and what skills will be needed. If it's urgent you'll need to pass it to whoever has the time, the skills and the experience to do it quickly. If it's not so urgent, you might want to give it to someone who is not necessarily the obvious choice – on the grounds that it will help him/her to acquire some new skill or gain some new experience. As a manager, you need to produce short-term results—to get the work done as effectively and efficiently as you can—but you also need to take every opportunity to develop the longer term potential of your team.

Don't just delegate the boring stuff

One of the perks of being a manager is the ability to delegate work that is really boring! But don't overdo it. A manager who always keeps all the interesting stuff for himself/herself won't be very popular with the team. If a member of your team has been carrying out a succession of routine tasks, find something you can delegate that's more interesting and more challenging.

Leave them to get on with it

When you delegate, give people as much rein as you can. Make very clear what you want done and set the parameters (e.g. deadline, quality standards, resources). But—and this is a cardinal rule of delegation—leave the person to whom you are delegating to decide how it will be done. Give them any necessary back-up (e.g. documents, speaking to or emailing heads of the departments they'll need to contact) and check that they understand the task. Then stand back and let them get on with it.

Fight for your team

It's important to fight for your team. You should be their champion, both inside and outside the organisation. Look after their interests, and pull out all the stops in getting them the best resources. If you don't, they'll see what others get, they'll resent it, and they'll be demotivated. If you want your team to be the best, treat them as the best.

Give them the credit – but take the blame

Let the team take all the credit. It really helps to motivate them – and, as their manager, some of it is bound to rub off on you anyway. On the other hand, if the team makes a mess of things, take the blame yourself. After all, it's your team. And nothing generates more loyalty.

Know when to stand back

It's an art rather than a science – knowing when to step in and when to leave the team to get on with it. If the team leader is constantly intervening and interfering it's bound to affect the team's confidence. Remember that people often learn more from their mistakes than they do from their successes. Seeing that you believe in them and trust them will work wonders for their confidence.

Reward success

If the team has had a big success, it's important to recognise and reward it. How you do that will depend to some extent on the culture of your organisation. Any financial rewards will be determined by the organisation's use of performance pay, special bonuses and so on. Regardless of that, the team leader needs to make a point of congratulating people – and making sure that any major success is recognised and acknowledged more widely within the organisation. If success means a feather in the cap for the team leader, he/she should not begrudge treating the team to a celebratory drink or meal. And if the team have put in a superhuman effort without getting the result you wanted, you can still reward them for the effort.

Make sure they know what's expected of them

People need to know what's expected of them. Setting clear tasks and objectives is an important part of that. But the manager also has a responsibility to make sure that his/her people understand the organisation's culture and the standards of conduct and behaviour that are expected. Of course, the very best way to do this is to model the kind of behaviour you are seeking to inculcate into others.

Train and develop your team

Take training and development seriously. Training is about helping your team to acquire or improve the skills they need to do the current job. Development is about helping them to move on – to learn the skills and gain the experience they'll need in the next job and beyond. Identifying training and development needs should be an integral part of the annual performance appraisal. Training courses can help, especially if they are based on learning by doing and are focussed on specific work-related needs.

But consider other options: sitting someone alongside a more experienced colleague, whether it's for a couple of days or just a couple of hours; job swaps; away-days where the team can learn from one another, perhaps by tackling a problematic issue; outside visits that enable people to see how their work fits into the wider context; secondments; or special one-off projects that provide new experience or an opportunity to learn new skills.

Coaching is another option. A coach is usually a training and development expert who helps on a one-to-one basis, typically with questions along the following lines:

- What's the problem – what do you want to achieve here?
- What's the background – what are the facts?
- What are your options?
- What action can you take, and how can obstacles be overcome?

A good coach helps the individual to find out what works for him/her.

Don't ignore conflict

Don't ignore conflict. It needs to be addressed and worked through. Conflict can arise for any number of reasons. There may be strong differences of opinion about the way the team operates or about the way a specific problem or project is being handled – or just clashes of personality. Whatever the reason, the team leader needs to grasp the nettle and talk it through with the rest of the team. That may be uncomfortable, but once it has been done the team will be stronger and healthier and will have a much better chance of achieving its objectives.

Help the team to grow

Begin by working with the team on problems that immediately resonate with team members. This will help to build trust and understanding. In doing that, the team will gradually learn how to make optimum use of their diverse experience and expertise and different perspectives. It will help the team to grow.

Don't force the team to adopt an approach

Sometimes you'll need to get your team to do something they don't really like. That's life: we can't spend all our time just doing the things we enjoy. But try not to force them to use a method or a system or an approach to which they are fundamentally opposed. If they don't really believe in it, the chances are they won't put in 100% effort. Make sure they know the result you're expecting them to produce but, if you possibly can, leave them to decide how they'll get there.

Money isn't everything

Very few people are motivated mainly by money. That may come as a surprise, but it's true. For most people, job satisfaction, security of employment, status and recognition, feeling appreciated, and prospects for future advancement are all more important than the salary. So don't feel that if you can't give your team more money, you can't motivate them. There are many, many other ways.

Make them feel good

Praise and encouragement are strong motivators. If the team have performed well, tell them. A few warm words can go a long way. If you make people feel good about themselves, they will be much more likely to have a positive attitude to their work and to perform to their utmost ability. You don't even have to wait until they have performed well to praise them! Tell them in advance how brilliant they are and how lucky you are to have such a great team. Then they won't want to let you—or themselves—down.

Chapter summary

- A team is a group of people with complementary skills, experience and roles, who work together to achieve common and agreed aims.

- Every member of the team must be clear about the team's objectives and about what he/she is expected to contribute.

- Team objectives should be SMART (specific, measurable, agreed, realistic and time-limited).

- Belbin's nine team roles or personality profiling models based on Jung's work can help you to understand differences in working styles.

- Apply the key principles of individual performance appraisal set out at pages 108/109.

- Lead by example.

- Remember that every manager who has staff management responsibilities is a leader.

- Get to know what makes each member of your team tick.

- Take every opportunity to train and develop your team.

- Praise your team and make them feel good about themselves.

Motivation is the art of getting people to do what you want them to do because they want to do it.

Dwight Eisenhower

Managing negotiations

Getting a result, and not just for today

chapter 8
Managing negotiations

Sooner or later, you're likely to find yourself involved in negotiations of one kind or another – perhaps over such things as budgets, pay, staffing, office accommodation and so on. There may be disagreements about policies or priorities, or demarcation disputes between different departments. These are not always called "negotiations", but very often you'll find that in order to arrive at a solution which everyone can accept, you need to settle for less than you would ideally like. You need to give and take, in other words, to negotiate.

These days most organisations contract out a whole range of support services – things like office cleaning, travel, transport, IT support, training, security, catering and so on. Someone has to negotiate all those contracts. If you're in sales you probably have to negotiate with customers or agents about prices, delivery dates, commission rates, etc. If your organisation has overseas operations or interests you may find yourself involved in international negotiations. For example, many organisations have European interests and are affected by developments in the European Union.

These scenarios are all very different, but the principles and techniques of effective negotiation apply to all of them.

Think long term

If you're buying a second-hand car, or arguing with a salesman at the door, or haggling over a piece of junk at a car boot sale, negotiating is pretty straightforward. You just decide how much you are prepared to pay. Then you offer less than that. Your sole aim is to get the best deal you can. If you're able to persuade the seller to accept less than you know the object is worth, you'll probably feel very pleased with yourself.

When a manager is negotiating, things are rather different. It doesn't matter whether the negotiation is internal or with an external contractor or other organisation. Shafting the opposition is unlikely to be a good idea. You'll almost certainly have to deal with them in the future. You need to get the best deal you can, of course, but it's usually advisable to ensure that the other party also gets something out of the negotiation. If you can do that, you'll have a much better chance of building a long-term, mutually beneficial relationship.

Know what your objective is

The first principle of negotiation is to be absolutely clear about your objective – what is it that you want to get out of it? Sounds obvious, doesn't it? But if it's a tricky or a very complex subject and you're pressed for time, it's all too easy to arrive at a meeting with only a very fuzzy idea of what it is that you are seeking. And that's a recipe for disaster. Of course, it's possible that you'll have to modify your objective – for example, if some new information comes to light, or if you're faced with facts or arguments which make it unsustainable. But it's imperative to begin with a very clear idea about what you want to achieve.

Make sure you have a fall-back position – and a bottom line

Whatever the ideal outcome is that you are seeking, the chances are that you won't get it! So you need to have a realistic fall-back position – something you could live with which you believe has a realistic chance of being acceptable to the other parties to the negotiation. You may need to do some detective work so that you can make an educated guess about others' negotiating positions.

Finally, work out your bottom line – the absolute minimum that you can accept. This is the line in the sand beyond which you will not go, whatever concessions are offered or whatever pleas or threats are made. This is the point at which you refuse to be party to any agreement.

Recognise reality

Clarity about your objective and your negotiating position—the ideal outcome, the fall-back and the bottom line—is the first (but only the first) step in preparing for any negotiation. At this point I feel the need to inject a dose of hard reality, based on personal experience. For six years I was the UK's representative to one of the Council Working Groups that meet in Brussels to hammer out differences between members of the European Union. I was involved in lots of negotiations, and there were often huge differences between the participants. On only one occasion did I get close to achieving the ideal outcome. Usually, the result was somewhere between the fall-back position and the bottom line – and it was often closer to the bottom line!

Make sure your negotiating position has been agreed

If the subject of the negotiation is of minor importance, or if the result will affect only you and your team, you can probably work out your negotiating position without reference to anyone else. But if your role is to represent your department, you need to make sure that your negotiating stance has been agreed by key stakeholders in the department. The same applies, to an even greater extent, if you are representing your whole organisation. You'll almost certainly need to have some internal discussions and negotiations in order to get all the key people on board and signed up to an agreed line.

These internal negotiations are sometimes the most difficult of all. When I worked at the Department of Trade and Industry and represented UK interests at EU negotiations in Brussels, the preparatory discussions between different Whitehall departments, thrashing out an agreed UK negotiating position, were sometimes more difficult than the subsequent negotiations in Brussels.

Make sure they've got a negotiating mandate

There are few things more frustrating to a negotiator than to discover that the person(s) he/she is negotiating with does not have the authority to agree to anything! It's bad enough if this is discovered at the outset of a meeting, but even worse if it emerges only at the end of the negotiation, after you thought you had a done deal.

Sometimes it might be appropriate and useful to have preparatory discussions, perhaps at a lower level, at which the parties to the negotiation can exchange preliminary views and see how much common ground there is, before the negotiations proper begin. But if that is the case, everyone needs to be crystal clear about the basis of the discussions. If you're a negotiator, you need to have a mandate to negotiate.

Find out what the others think

To negotiate effectively you need to know something about the negotiating position of the people on the other side of the table. That's not always easy, but more often than not a glance at the relevant papers or a few phone calls will throw some light on the approach they are likely to adopt. If you can get some clues about their attitude, you should be able to make some sort of guess about the points they're likely to make and to think about how you can deal with them.

Probe beneath the surface

Those you are negotiating with will probably take up a position and use all the facts and arguments they can muster to defend that position. If it's an important negotiation the line they take will have been agreed at a high level within their organisation, and they may have little or no room for manoeuvre. They're unlikely to say much, if anything, about what lies behind their negotiating position. In order to have any realistic chance of persuading them to change that position, you need to probe beneath the surface. You need to understand the pressures they are under and the interests and concerns they are seeking to protect.

Almost certainly, you won't be able to do that during the negotiation itself – especially if there are lots of participants, all representing different interests and all with different axes to grind. No-one is likely to be particularly forthcoming in front of a big audience.

Have a quiet tête-à-tête

On the other hand, if you can have a quiet chat, one-to-one, with the main parties to the negotiation, they may well be prepared to be a little more open about the pressures they are under and the underlying concerns and interests they are seeking to protect. Obviously, if you're going on a fishing expedition for this kind of information, you'll have to be prepared to say something about the interests and concerns behind your own negotiating position. But that's what's involved in any negotiation – you have to give as well as to take.

Get to know them

It's easier to negotiate if you know the people you're negotiating with. So take the trouble to get to know them. Arrive a few minutes early so that you can have an informal word with people before the serious business begins. Even if you're just exchanging pleasantries or chatting about the latest political scandal, it can help to break the ice. If you can establish some kind of personal rapport with the people around the table, you'll probably feel more relaxed and this will make it easier for you to get your points across. It will also help to promote the kind of friendly, constructive atmosphere in which any negotiation is most likely to succeed.

Use informal contacts

The more negotiations I was involved with in Brussels, the more I realised the value of informal contacts and quiet, one-to-one discussions. Sometimes these took place in the corner of the meeting room, but more often it was over a coffee or a beer or over lunch in the canteen.

When negotiations became really difficult and there were huge differences of approach, it was very rare that these differences were settled in the conference room. More often, informal, often bilateral, discussions eventually resulted in some softening of positions and enabled the deadlock to be broken. If you are dealing with complex issues, this can be a slow, painstaking process. But whether the negotiation is simple and straightforward or complex and difficult, informal contacts and one-to-one discussions are often the key to success.

Know your stuff – prepare thoroughly

Make sure, before you go into the negotiation, that you have a real understanding of the subject matter. Take time to brief yourself thoroughly. You'll need to look at previous papers or reports; you may need to talk to colleagues who've been involved in the past; or to consult experts or specialists, inside or outside your organisation, who know more about the subject than you do.

Make sure that you have all the relevant facts and figures at your fingertips, and that you really know your stuff. The better prepared you are, the greater your chances of success.

Use your meeting and presentation skills

Some of the tips given in Chapter 3 (Managing Presentations) and Chapter 4 (Managing Meetings) apply also to negotiations. You need to get your points across clearly and succinctly. You need to make an impact. You need to listen very carefully to what others are saying: you may need to read between the lines. If you don't understand something, ask questions and seek clarification. When you speak yourself, try to use specific examples to back up your arguments.

Know when to listen and when to speak

You need to think about when and how you intervene in the discussion. You might want to get in early so that you can set the agenda, influence the direction of the discussion, and focus on those aspects that are of particular importance to you. Or you might want to keep your powder dry: to hear what others have to say first, so that you are in a better position to counter their arguments. Based on your negotiating objective and on what you know about the objectives of other people around the table, you have to decide which tactics will enable you to make your case most effectively. It's your call.

Watch out for linkages

At high-level negotiations, when the stakes are high, linkages may be made, especially during the end-game, between totally unrelated issues: "OK, we've reached agreement on X. But I'm only going to sign up to it if you give me what I want on Y." A linkage of that kind can be difficult to deal with. The best hope of avoiding or dealing effectively with it is probably:

- having an in-depth understanding of the interests and motivations of your negotiating partner;

- close personal contacts and a good rapport with your negotiating partner;

- a clear understanding of the importance your organisation attaches to the issue on which you're negotiating and of how it fits into the bigger picture of the organisation's overall interests;

- to be armed with an unrelated demand of your own which you can use as bargaining counter in the event of any attempted last-minute linkage.

Be clear about what has been agreed

At the end of the negotiation it's vital for everyone to have a clear, agreed understanding of what has (and, perhaps, what has not) been agreed. Someone needs to sum up the result, going through everything that has been agreed in as much detail as is necessary to avoid any possibility of misunderstanding. Negotiations at the very highest levels sometimes break up with different participants having a rather different understanding of what has been agreed! Make sure this does not happen to you.

Take care to ensure that the detail of exactly what has been agreed is recorded in writing and circulated to all the participants. It's best for this to be done immediately the negotiation is concluded, even if the detail has to be incorporated into a formal contract, agreement or other document that will be drawn up at a later date.

Chapter summary

- Be clear about your negotiating objective.

- Get the best deal you can, but look to build a long-term relationship.

- Have a fall-back position and a bottom line.

- Find out as much as you can about others' negotiating positions.

- Probe beneath the surface to identify the interests your negotiating partners are seeking to promote or protect.

- Get to know the people you're negotiating with.

- Informal one-to-one discussions are often the key to success.

- Make sure you are well prepared, and have all the relevant facts and arguments at your fingertips.

- Use your meeting and presentation skills to argue your case as clearly, succinctly and convincingly as you can.

- Make sure you know what's been agreed and get it recorded in writing.

> "My main job was developing talent. I was a gardener providing water and other nourishment to our top 750 people. Of course, I had to pull out some weeds, too.

Jack Welch

Managing decisions

It's no good shirking them

chapter 9
Managing decisions

Taking decisions comes with the territory: if you're a manager, you can't avoid them. Some, such as approving someone's holiday plans or expense claims, are minor; and some are major – for example, deciding whether to go ahead with an important project, or recruiting a key member of your team. Some are easy and some are difficult. Some can be taken quickly and some require a great deal of thought and, perhaps, consultation with others. Decisions come in all shapes and sizes.

The more senior you are, the more decisions you're likely to have to take, and the more critical and difficult they'll be. As you progress higher up the organisation, it becomes ever more important to see the big picture – to take account of the wider political, economic, social and environmental context. If you get to the very top, you'll be taking decisions that have a major impact on your organisation and those who work for it – and, quite probably, on the outside world.

If you have to take a tricky decision, put your subjective thoughts to one side and consider the matter objectively and professionally, on the basis of the facts.

Effective decision-making requires experience, common sense and good judgement.

Make sure it's your decision to take

Before you take the decision, make sure you are the right person to take it. Is the subject matter one in which another part of your organisation has a greater interest? If so, it may be more sensible to get someone in another department to take the decision, feeding in any relevant facts or arguments you may have. If the decision clearly falls within your bailiwick, consider whether it's one you can delegate to a member of your team. Or perhaps it's a decision your boss will expect to take, or at least to be consulted about? If that's the case, try to get into the habit of giving him/her your own views and saying what decision you recommend.

Do you need to consult?

Once you're clear that you are the right person to take the decision, think about whether or not you need to consult others. That will depend upon (a) the complexity of the subject-matter and (b) who will be affected by it. You might need to seek the views of other members of your team, or to consult people elsewhere in the organisation – or outside.

Think about how you consult

If you do need to consult others, take a moment to consider the best way of doing this. In some cases a simple phone call might suffice. If the issue is more substantive or more complex, you'll probably need to seek views in writing, perhaps by email. In this event, it's always advisable to set a deadline. If you conclude that the issue needs thorough discussion, you may need to call a meeting.

Identify the options

If the decision is a simple one, there may be only two options: to say either yes or no. If it's more complex, there may be several possible reactions. If that's the case, you need to weigh up the options before you take a decision.

The first thing to do is to identify all the possible ways of dealing with the problem. One way of doing this is to brainstorm the issue – to get together with your team and/or your colleagues who are most involved, and come up with as many options as possible. Don't try to evaluate these during the brainstorming session itself. Just let ideas flow as fast and as freely as you can, however impracticable or off-the-wall they might be.

Once the initial brainstorming session has ended, stand back and allow people to discuss the ideas they've come up with. At this point you'll probably agree to dismiss some of them out of hand. But someone's apparently crazy idea might light a spark in someone else, stimulating discussion and perhaps leading to the identification of something that could really work. With any luck you'll end up with a short list of viable options.

Identify the pros and cons

Once you have identified the options, you need to consider each one in turn, identifying its pros and cons. For each option, there are bound to be both advantages and disadvantages. Just put them all down methodically, either on paper or on a flip chart.

Establish criteria and evaluate the options

Once you have identified the options and listed the pros and cons of each one, you need to weigh them, one against the other. To do this, you need to establish criteria – to decide which factors you will take into account in comparing one option with another. The criteria you select will depend on the subject-matter. They might, for example, include such things as cost, practicability, acceptability to staff, stakeholder reactions and speed of implementation.

It's often the case that some criteria are more important than others. You can reflect this by giving a different weighting to each of your chosen criteria, perhaps using a scale of 1-5. Then you can evaluate each of your options according to the extent to which it satisfies or does not satisfy each of the criteria, perhaps awarding points on a scale of 0-10. If you multiply the latter by the weighting given to each criterion, you'll be able to see which of your options best meets your criteria.

But don't be over-reliant on the arithmetic. If there is not much to choose between, say, your top two or three options, don't be afraid to be guided, in the final analysis, by experience and common sense – and sheer gut instinct.

Which stakeholders will be affected by the decision?

Before you take a final decision, think through what effect it will have on your key stakeholders. You might want to glance back at Chapter 5 (Managing Projects) and use the stakeholder analysis techniques described there. Once you are clear about

" There are no problems that we cannot solve together, and very few that we can solve by ourselves "

Lyndon Johnson

who the stakeholders are and how they will be affected by your decision, you can consider how to handle them. You might want to seek their views or even to involve them in the decision-making process.

Identify the risks

Some decisions are routine and virtually risk-free. But if it's an important decision, it's worthwhile considering what, if any, risks are involved. If the decision does involve significant risks, you can analyse these for probability and impact, as described in Chapter 5. If you conclude that the risks of your preferred decision are just too great, you might have to consider alternative options. If you decide that all the possible options involve unacceptable risks, you'll have to think about the risks involved in taking no decision.

Think about the consequences – then get on with it

Once you have reached a decision, think through the consequences before you put it into effect. Try to get into the habit of doing this as a matter of course, however big or small the decision. If you're tempted to put it off, think about the consequences of doing that!

Then put your decision into effect without delay. Don't prevaricate. In the long run, the downside of putting off difficult decisions is often worse than the consequences of taking decisive action. Even if people don't agree with your decision, they'll probably respect you for taking it.

Think creatively

If you're faced with a difficult decision, it's sensible to look at how similar issues or problems have been dealt with in the past. Think about who may have been faced with this problem before. Sometimes the precedent will provide the answer, but it's not a good idea to be constrained by what happened in the past. The circumstances may have changed. Look at the issue with a fresh pair of eyes. Think laterally.

Communicate your decision

Don't forget to communicate your decision to those affected by it. Lack of effective communication is one of the commonest causes of misunderstandings and confusion in any organisation. If people aren't told about a decision that affects them, you'll store up trouble for the future. Think carefully about how and when to communicate it.

Make sure the decision is put into effect

It's often easier to take a decision than to ensure that it is implemented effectively. Make sure that the necessary follow-up action is taken. Don't assume that once you have taken the decision, that's the end of the matter. It might only be the beginning!

If the decision is a substantive one (for example, initiating a new policy, project or working procedures) you may need to use project management techniques to ensure that it is implemented effectively.

Chapter summary

- Experience, common sense and good judgement are the main prerequisites for effective decision-making.

- Make sure you're the right person to take the decision.

- Consider the need to consult others.

- Identify the options, and consider the pros and cons of each one.

- Evaluate the options using common criteria.

- Consider the risks (if any) and their probability and potential impact.

- Consider the consequences, and think about how stakeholders will be affected.

- Don't put off difficult decisions: the downside can be worse than the consequences of taking decisive action.

- Pay attention to the way your decision is communicated.

- Take steps to ensure that the decision is implemented effectively.

What I hear, I forget; what I see, I remember; but what I do, I understand.

Confucius 551-479 BC

Managing change

You can't avoid it

chapter 10
Managing change

Change is inevitable. To survive and prosper, an organisation needs to improve continuously and to adapt to the changing world around it. If it doesn't change, it can't improve.

On the other hand, constant change and reorganisation does more harm than good. Institutional memory is lost, everyone worries about their future rather than the job they're doing, and no-one really understands what's happening.

Increasingly, however, whether we like it or loathe it, change is the norm. It's worth remembering that it does not necessarily have to mean massive upheaval. Relatively small adjustments to the way things are done can sometimes result in a significant cumulative improvement in effectiveness and efficiency.

Most people find change unsettling, and major organisational change can be a tough challenge for any manager. It has to be handled sensitively. The ability to adapt, and to help others to adapt, to changed circumstances is one of the hallmarks of an effective manager.

There are countless models of change management, and a couple of these (Kotter and McKinsey) are mentioned briefly in this chapter. Personally, I'm not a great fan of models. They often look better on paper than when you try to put them into practice in the real world. But they can be useful as a reminder of key issues to think about or steps to take.

Pay attention to four key principles

If you have to implement a programme of major organisational change, there are four key themes you need to think about:

- Leadership
- Communication
- Strategy
- Culture

If you don't have a clear understanding of each of these you'll have an uphill struggle.

Leadership is critical

No programme of change has much chance of success unless those at the top of the organisation are committed to it. I have been involved in change programmes, both in the UK and in Central and Eastern Europe, which have failed to produce the results expected simply because, at the end of the day, those at the very top were not committed to them. It's not sufficient for top management to go along passively with a change programme: they need to be proactively involved in promoting it, putting it into practice, and modelling the changed actions or behaviours they want others to adopt.

Leadership does not stop at the top

Every manager needs to lead the people he/she manages. If you're implementing major changes, you must explain and sell those changes to your team. Show by your own example that you're committed to putting them into practice and give your people whatever help and support they need.

Look at change as an opportunity, not a threat

The chances are, you won't like every aspect of the changes you have to implement. Perhaps you won't like anything at all about them! Try to look at them—and to get your team to look at them—not as a threat, but as an opportunity. Whatever the nature of the changes, there are bound to be some positive elements. Home in on these. Instead of reacting defensively and negatively, think positively. Encourage your people to make the most of the opportunity to do things differently. It could give them the chance to demonstrate skills they didn't even know they had.

Communication, communicate, communicate.

Whatever kind of change you're involved with, communicating that change effectively to those who're affected is critically important. And this can be a tricky business, especially if people are not convinced that the change will be in their best interests. They need to understand the rationale – to know why the change is taking place and what it is intended to achieve. They need to know how and when it will be implemented, what effect it will have on them, what the benefits will be, and exactly what their own role will be in putting it into practice.

Stakeholder involvement is critical

It's imperative to keep your major stakeholders informed and involved. If you don't, and they dislike the changes you're making, they'll cause trouble.

Change needs to be bottom-up

Commitment from those at the top of the organisation is a prerequisite for successful change. But if the change is to be more than surface-deep it also needs to be embraced by those at the coalface lower down the organisation. Staff with practical, day-to-day experience of operational issues often know better than anyone else how to implement change most effectively; and change brought about with the active participation and involvement of the workforce will be far more firmly-rooted than anything imposed from above. So do your utmost to involve people in the practical details of how the changes are put into practice on the ground. Give them some responsibility, and the chances are they'll feel some ownership.

Know the strategy – where you're going

In any change situation, it's important for people to have a clear understanding of the organisation's strategic direction – to know where it is going and how it's going to get there. And your team needs to understand how they fit into the strategy. Then, with any luck, everyone will pull in the same direction.

Cultural change is difficult – focus on the little things

Organisational culture is a difficult thing to define. It's really an amalgam of "the way things are done around here." It includes such things as values, beliefs, structure, control mechanisms, rituals, routines, symbols and language.

> It is not the strongest of the species that survive, nor the most intelligent, but the most responsive to change.

Charles Darwin

Changing processes and systems is relatively straightforward: it might take time for people to get to grips with new procedures, but with training and on-the-job support it does not usually present insuperable problems. Organisational culture is more intangible and difficult to pin down. For this reason cultural change is hard to tackle head-on. It's often easier and more productive to focus on the little things — for example, the kinds of behaviour and day-to-day routines which the organisation is seeking to encourage.

Certainly, cultural change is unlikely to be achieved through lecturing or evangelising. The key influences are more likely to be role models, peer pressure and clear leadership: as ever, those at the top need to "walk the talk".

Pilot it first

It's only common sense to pilot any major change. Try it first on a small scale to see how it works. The chances are you'll need to make a few changes, or at least to fine tune some of the detail. When you have applied the lessons learnt from the pilot, you're more likely to end up with something that will really work. Then you can roll it out across the board. Sustainability is more important than speed.

Copy the best

You don't need to be original. Often all you need to do is to identify the best — and to copy it! This is how many famous painters, musicians and writers learnt their craft. If you come across something that someone else is doing that really works, don't hesitate to copy it.

If you like models, try Kotter

John Kotter is author of the book *Leading Change* (1996). His model of change management has 8 steps, summarised as follows:

1. Create a sense of urgency.

2. Set up a small, powerful group committed to change.

3. Build a clear view of the desired future.

4. Embody that view in day-to-day activities.

5. Encourage and empower employees to implement change.

6. Ensure some quick wins.

7. Use short-term successes as stepping stones to change.

8. Fix the change as permanent.

Or consider McKinsey's 7S framework

This model identifies 7 factors which managers seeking to implement change should take into account. These are: strategy, shared values, staff, skills, style, systems, and structure. It's a way of making sure that you look at change in an organisation from many different angles and perspectives.

The start and the finish

Successful change demands clear analysis of three questions:

- Where are we now?
- Where do we want to get to?
- What is the gap, and how can we bridge it?

Chapter summary

- If an organisation doesn't change, it can't improve.
- Look at change as an opportunity, not a threat.
- Adapting to change—and helping others to adapt—is one of the hallmarks of an effective manager.
- Pay attention to four key themes – leadership, communication, strategic direction, and culture.
- Successful change requires both leadership from the top and involvement by those at the coalface.
- Models of change management can help you to identify critical issues and key steps.
- Be clear about where you are now and where you want to get to.

Put at least one of these tips into practice!

That's the end of *The Greatest Management Tips in the World*. Most of them are plain common sense. You'll forget some of them – and you'll probably think that others are so basic that you don't need to remember them. But if you put just one of these tips into practice—and that helps you to be a more effective manager—this book will have been worth writing.

Recommended reading

Team Roles at Work
by R. Meredith Belbin (Butterworth-Heinemann, 2003)

Management Teams: Why They Succeed or Fail
by R. Meredith Belbin (Butterworth-Heinemann, 2003)

Introduction to Type
by Isabel Briggs Myers (Consulting Psychologists Press, 1998)

Working with Emotional Intelligence
by Daniel Coleman (Bloomsbury, 1999)

Leading Change
by John P. Kotter (Harvard Business School Press, 1996)

The 80/20 Principle: The Secret of Achieving More with Less
by Richard Koch (Nicholas Brealey Publishing, 2007)

The Effective Executive: The Definitive Guide to Getting the Right Things Done
by Peter F. Drucker (Harper Collins, 2006)

The 7 Habits of Highly Effective People
by Stephen R. Covey (Simon and Shuster, 1999)

Embracing Change – Essential Steps to Make Your Future Today
by Tony Buzan (BBC Books, 2005)

Developing your Career in Management
Jeremy G. Thorn (Mercury Books, 1992)

How to be a Civil Servant
by Martin Stanley (Politoco's Publishing, 2000)

Index

A

Action, taking, 32
Agendas, 56
Appraising, 108-110

B

Blame, 21
Boss, 16-17
Breaks, 33

C

Chairing a meeting, 57-61
Change, 146-153
Communication, 84-97, 142, 148
Communication, written, 89-93
Conflict, 119
Consequences, 141
Consultation, 137
Contact list, 11
Cultural change, 149, 151
Customers, 22

D

Deadlines, 29
Decisions, 136-143
Delegation, 115-16

E

Emails, 93, 96
Encouragement, 120
Energy, 34
Enthusiasm, 12
Evaluation, 139
Eye contact, 43

F

Flip chart, 44

G

Gannt chart, 78

H

Honesty, 13, 86
Humour, 15

I

Impact, 73
Influencing, 18
Internet, 97

J

Jargon, 96

K

Kotter, John, 152

L

Leadership, 110-111, 147
Linkages, 131-132
Listening, 22, 131
Lists, 29

M

Management by walking
about (MBWA), 11
Meetings, 32, 53-67
Meetings, bad, 65
Meetings, effective, 64
Mentor, 18
Milestones, 79

N

Negotiating position, 127-128
Negotiations, 124-133
Networking, 11
Networks, 11
Note-taking, 63

O

Objectives, presentation, 40
Objectives, negotiation,
125-126
Obstacles, 73, 75
Options, 138, 139

Outcome, 76
Output, 76

P

Pareto principle, 27
Passion, 16
People, 10-23
Performance criteria, 79
Personal plan, 19
Persuading, 18
PowerPoint, 45
Praise, 120
Preparation, 38, 55, 130
Presentations, 38-51
Presentation, bad, 50
Presentation length, 46
Priorities, 28, 29
Probability, 73
Project management
software, 80
Projects, 70-81
Punctuality, 34

Q

Questions, 12, 48

R

Reactivity, 31

Reading, recommended, 154
Rehearsing a presentation, 49
Reports, 56
Rewards, 117
Risks, 73, 75, 141

S

Speaking, 38-51
Stakeholders, 71-73, 139, 141, 148
Strategy, 149

T

Team characteristics, 103
Team communication, 87
Team development, 101-104, 118
Team objectives, 104
Team player, 113
Team roles, 105
Teams, 100-121
Temper, 21
Terminology, project, 77
Time management, 26-35
Time wasting, 27, 31
Training, 118

U

Urgency, 28

V

Visual aids, 44

W

Websites, 97

'The Greatest Tips in the World' books

Baby & Toddler Tips
ISBN 978-1-905151-70-7

Barbeque Tips
ISBN 978-1-905151-68-4

Breastfeeding Tips
ISBN 978-1-905151-34-0

Cat Tips
ISBN 978-1-905151-66-0

Collecting Tips
ISBN 978-1-905151-42-4

Cookery Tips
ISBN 978-1-905151-64-6

Cricketing Tips
ISBN 978-1-905151-18-9

DIY Tips
ISBN 978-1-905151-62-2

Dog Tips
ISBN 978-1-905151-67-7

Etiquette & Dining Tips
ISBN 978-1-905151-21-9

Fishing Tips
ISBN 978-1-905151-32-2

Freelance Writing Tips
ISBN 978-1-905151-17-2

Gardening Tips
ISBN 978-1-905151-60-8

Genealogy Tips
ISBN 978-1-905151-72-1

Golfing Tips
ISBN 978-1-905151-63-9

Horse & Pony Tips
ISBN 978-1-905151-19-6

Household Tips
ISBN 978-1-905151-61-5

Life Coaching Tips
ISBN 978-1-905151-23-3

Management Tips
ISBN 978-1-905151-44-8

Marketing Tips
ISBN 978-1-905151-41-7

Moving Abroad Tips
ISBN 978-1-905151-47-9

Personal Success Tips
ISBN 978-1-905151-71-4

Photography Tips
ISBN 978-1-905151-39-4

Podcasting Tips
ISBN 978-1-905151-75-2

Property Developing Tips
ISBN 978-1-905151-69-1

Relationship & Dating Tips
ISBN 978-1-905151-35-6

Retirement Tips
ISBN 978-1-905151-28-8

Sales Tips
ISBN 978-1-905151-40-0

Sex Tips
ISBN 978-1-905151-74-5

Travel Tips
ISBN 978-1-905151-73-8

Slimming & Healthy Living Tips
ISBN 978-1-905151-31-8

Wedding Tips
ISBN 978-1-905151-27-1

Tax Tips
ISBN 978-1-905151-43-1

Pet Recipe books

The Greatest Feline Feasts in the World
ISBN 978-1-905151-50-9

The Greatest Doggie Dinners in the World
ISBN 978-1-905151-51-6

'The Greatest in the World' DVDs

The Greatest in the World – Gardening Tips

The Greatest in the World – Yoga Tips

The Greatest in the World – Cat & Kitten Tips

The Greatest in the World – Dog & Puppy Tips

For more information about currently available
and forthcoming book and DVD titles please visit:

www.thegreatestintheworld.com

or write to:

The Greatest in the World Ltd
PO Box 3182
Stratford-upon-Avon
Warwickshire CV37 7XW
United Kingdom

Tel / Fax: +44(0)1789 299616
Email: info@thegreatestintheworld.com

The author

Tony Rossiter is a freelance consultant, trainer and writer with more than 40 years' experience of management.

He is currently a Director of Studies for courses on management, policy development and strategic change at RIPA International. His recent work has included management training in Nigeria, Moldova and Kosovo, development of a staff appraisal system in Ukraine, and training in communication skills (chairing meetings, writing reports) for the Council of Europe in Strasbourg.

He has held a wide range of management jobs, including diplomatic posts in Moscow, Karachi and Buenos Aires. From 1991-97 he was UK representative on a European Union Council Working Group, and from 1997-2004 Principal International Consultant at the National School of Government, where he directed and contributed to public administration reform projects in the UK and in many parts of Central and Eastern Europe.

Tony can be contacted at: tonyrossiter06@aol.com